The Princeton Review

Are You Ready for the
SAT®
& ACT®?

Building Critical Reading Skills
for Rising High School Students
2nd Edition

The Staff of The Princeton Review

PrincetonReview.com

Penguin Random House

The Princeton Review, Inc.
24 Prime Parkway, Suite 201
Natick, MA 01760
E-mail: editorialsupport@review.com

Published in the United States by Penguin Random House LLC, New York, and in Canada by Random House of Canada, a division of Penguin Random House Ltd., Toronto.

Terms of Service: The Princeton Review Online Companion Tools ("Student Tools") for retail books are available for only the two most recent editions of that book. Student Tools may be activated only twice per eligible book purchased for two consecutive 12-month periods, for a total of 24 months of access. Activation of Student Tools more than twice per book is in direct violation of these Terms of Service and may result in discontinuation of access to Student Tools Services.

ISBN: 978-1-101-88213-9
eBook ISBN: 978-1-101-88214-6
ISSN: 2332-8509

SAT is a registered trademark of the College Board, and ACT is a registered trademark of ACT, Inc., neither of which sponsors or endorses this product.

The Princeton Review is not affiliated with Princeton University.

Editor: Meave Shelton
Production Editor: Ali Landreau
Production Artist: Craig Patches

Printed in the United States of America on partially recycled paper.

10   9   8   7   6   5   4   3   2   1

Second Edition

Editorial
Rob Franek, Senior VP, Publisher
Casey Cornelius, VP Content Development
Mary Beth Garrick, Director of Production
Selena Coppock, Managing Editor
Meave Shelton, Senior Editor
Colleen Day, Editor
Sarah Litt, Editor
Aaron Riccio, Editor
Orion McBean, Editorial Assistant

Random House Publishing Team
Tom Russell, Publisher
Alison Stoltzfus, Publishing Manager
Melinda Ackell, Associate Managing Editor
Ellen Reed, Production Manager
Kristin Lindner, Production Supervisor
Andrea Lau, Designer

Acknowledgments

The Princeton Review would like to thank the following individuals for their contributions to this title: Elizabeth Owens, Lisa Mayo, Alice Swan, Brian Becker, Lori DesRochers, and Jonathan Chiu, National Content Director for High School Programs.

Special thanks to Adam Robinson, who conceived of and perfected the Joe Bloggs approach to standardized tests, and many of the other successful techniques used by The Princeton Review.

Contents

Register Your

1 Go to **PrincetonReview.com/cracking**

2 You'll see a welcome page where you can register your book using following ISBN: 9781101882139.

3 After placing this free order, you'll either be asked to log in or to answer a few simple questions in order to set up a new Princeton Review account.

4 Finally, click on the "Student Tools" tab located at the top of the screen. It may take an hour or two for your registration to go through, but after that, you're good to go.

NOTE: If you are experiencing book problems (potential content errors), please contact EditorialSupport@review.com with the full title of the book, its ISBN number (located above), and the page number of the error.

Experiencing technical issues? Please email TPRStudentTech@review.com with the following information:

- your full name
- e-mail address used to register the book
- full book title and ISBN
- your computer OS (Mac or PC) and Internet browser (Firefox, Safari, Chrome, etc.)
- description of technical issue

Book Online!

Once you've registered, you can...

- Download lined paper for the practice SAT and ACT essay prompts in this book
- Get valuable advice about the college application process, including tips for writing a great essay and where to apply for financial aid
- Check to see whether there have been any corrections to this edition

And for information on test changes, visit...

- PrincetonReview.com/SATChanges
- PrincetonReview.com/ACTChanges

The **Princeton** Review

Foreword

We at The Princeton Review are excited to present this publication as a means to improve critical reading and critical thinking skills. For those students who are just starting to hear about standardized tests, such as the ACT and the SAT, completing the activities in this book will greatly enhance their appreciation for the power of a single word and solidify their understanding of how sentences, paragraphs, and passages are constructed. Activities for everyone from novice readers to expert readers are spread throughout this book to develop skills that will be vital to success not only in high school but also in college and beyond.

To the students who will utilize this book to its fullest potential, we hope you enjoy this process of learning how to critically evaluate passages as much as we did in creating these fun activities.

Good luck in your academic journey!

—Jonathan Chiu, Ph.D.
National Content Director
High School Programs

Word Play

Author: Elizabeth Owens

Parts of Speech

Parts of speech are like the building blocks of sentences. Every word in a sentence has a function. Knowing the function of each word can help you figure out what's going on in a sentence. It can also help you to construct interesting and varied sentences.

There are 8 parts of speech.

1. **Nouns** are people, places, things, or ideas.
   a. Common nouns: *tree, store, badger, mummy*
   b. Proper nouns: *Frankenstein, Harry Potter, January, Rodeo Dr.*

2. **Verbs** express actions, events, or states of being.
   Ex: Malcolm *rode* the roller coaster. Malcolm *was* first in line.

3. **Adjectives** describe nouns.
   Ex: The *creepy* store sold *cheap* costumes.

4. **Adverbs** describe verbs, adjectives, or other adverbs.
   Ex: The cookie *quickly* disappeared. The chocolate was *extremely* delicious.

5. **Pronouns** replace nouns and make sentences less repetitive.
   a. Personal pronouns refer to specific people or things: *she, it, they*
   b. Demonstrative pronouns point to and identify a noun or pronoun: *this, that, these*
   c. Interrogative pronouns ask questions: *which, whom, what*

6. **Prepositions** link nouns, pronouns, and phrases to other words in a sentence. They give information about where the object is in space or time.
   Ex: The troll is *under* the bridge. The movie started *after* the previews.

Ron and Joe/Shutterstock.com

7. **Conjunctions** link words or phrases.
   Ex: *and, but, for, yet*

8. **Interjections** are used to express emotion.
   Ex: *Ouch! Hey! Oh.*

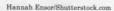

Hannah Ensor/Shutterstock.com

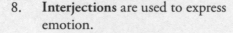

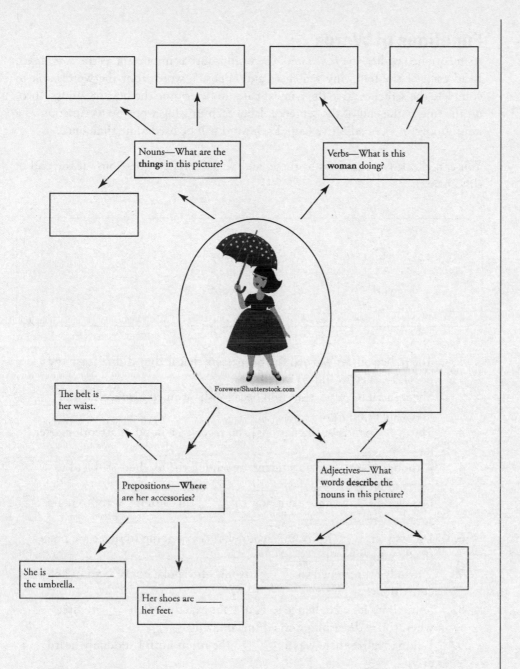

Nouns—What are the **things** in this picture?

Verbs—What is this **woman** doing?

Forewer/Shutterstock.com

The belt is _____ her waist.

Prepositions—**Where** are her accessories?

She is _____ the umbrella.

Her shoes are _____ her feet.

Adjectives—What words **describe** the nouns in this picture?

Functions of Words

As mentioned earlier, the *function* of the word is just as important as the *word* itself. Read each of the following sentences and choose a word from the word bank to complete the sentence. Use the context clues to determine the best meaning. Then, on the line at the end of the sentence, label each missing word by its function as a noun (n), verb (v), or adjective (adj). Each word will be used more than once.

You can check your answers to these, and all subsequent questions, at the end of this chapter.

> jail   baby
>
> work   word

1. The police officer warned the trespassers that if they didn't leave the property, they would go to <u>jail</u>.   _n_
2. She refused to _____ the child because she wanted him to learn to take care of himself. _____
3. The _____ panda at the national zoo received a flood of attention after its birth. _____
4. Although there were no students at school, the teachers still had to come in for the _____ day. _____
5. Can you help me figure out how to _____ this letter? I want to make sure I say this correctly. _____
6. Unless you _____ for NASA, your chances of going to space are practically non-existent. _____
7. The judge threatened to _____ anyone who spoke out of turn in her courtroom. _____
8. Sometimes it's a challenge to figure out exactly which _____ to use when you're describing something amazing. _____
9. I didn't realize there was a _____ in the room until I suddenly heard crying. _____
10. My favorite thing to do on a long car ride is to play _____ games. I'm particularly good at crossword puzzles and jumbles. _____

Fill in the Blanks

NOUN Adventure

Brainstorm some nouns and write down 8 of your favorites. Then transfer the nouns to the matching blanks in the paragraph on the next page and read about your crazy NOUN adventure!

1. _____

2. _____

3. _____

4. _____

5. _____

6. _____

7. _____

8. _____

VERB Afternoon

Brainstorm some verbs and write down 9 of your favorites. Be sure to pay attention to the tenses/endings. Then transfer the verbs to the matching blanks in the paragraph on the next page and read about your Saturday VERB Afternoon!

1. _____ (present tense)

2. _____ (present tense)

3. _____ (present tense, end with *-ing*)

4. _____ (present tense)

5. _____ (past tense)

6. _____ (past tense)

7. _____ (past tense)

8. _____ (present tense)

9. _____ (present tense, end with *-ing*)

NOUN Adventure

Last weekend, I packed my favorite _____ and two pairs of _____s and
                                              1   2
headed off on an adventure. I didn't have an exact plan, but I was hoping to see

a _____ or at least a _____. Unfortunately, less than an hour into my trip,
       3   4

I ran over a _____ and broke the _____ in my car. My dreams of ad-
                  5   6

venture disappeared in a puff of _____ when the repairman handed me a
                                         7

_____ for the cost of the repairs.
      8

VERB Afternoon

On Saturday, my best friend and I went out to _____ and then we went to see
                                                     1

a movie. I wanted to see the new romantic comedy, because I love watching two

people _____ in love. My friend really wanted to see the new action adventure,
            2

though, so we ended up _____ an explorer race to find a treasure before his
                              3

arch nemesis could _____ it. The hero _____ through the jungle, _____
                          4   5   6

through small European towns, and frantically _____ maps looking for clues.
                                                     7

Eventually, with the help of a fellow adventurer, he was able to _____ the trea-
                                                                        8

sure. And, to my delight, the two ended up _____ in love.
                                                  9

ADJECTIVE Holiday!

Brainstorm some solid, descriptive adjectives and write down 9 of your favorites on the lines below. Then transfer the adjectives to the matching blanks in the paragraph on the next page and read about your fabulous ADJECTIVE Holiday!

1. _____

2. _____

3. _____

4. _____

5. _____

6. _____

7. _____

8. _____

9. _____

ADJECTIVE Holiday!

My favorite time of the year is _____ time. The weather gets colder, there is

1

_____ music on the radio, and people walk around with _____ smiles on

2   3

their faces. I love to bake _____ cookies and make _____ candy. Our

4   5

_____ tree sparkles with _____ lights and decorations, and the stack of

6   7

_____ presents underneath steadily grows as we get closer and closer to the

8

_____ day.

9

Description Conniption

In the following paragraph, adjectives and adverbs are bolded. Read the paragraph carefully and decide which type of word is bolded in each case. Remember that adjectives only describe nouns, while adverbs can describe verbs, adjectives, or other adverbs. Adverbs often end with -ly, but not always! **Circle the adjectives and box the adverbs.**

The day of the **costume** contest had **finally** arrived. Mrs. Fuzzypaws woke with butterflies in her stomach. Or maybe that was just a hairball. No matter. Today was the day! She could feel it. This year was going to be her year. Tibsy had taken Grand Champion the **past two** years, first for her **outrageously clever** Catopatra outfit and then **last** year with her Queen Feline getup. Mrs. Fuzzypaws knew that **second** place was nothing to sneeze at, but she **desperately** wanted to win. And **this** year, she figured it was in the bag. Relevant, **well**-made, and clever, the **scarlet** and gold scarf had been knitted **precisely** to fit her neck, and the wig had **carefully** been curled and then frizzed. A **quick** lick of the paws, a clip of the nails, and she was ready to make her debut … as Purr-mione Granger.

Bring It All Together!

You have seen words function as various parts of speech. Now let's see how words can be changed from one part to another. Carefully read through the following chart and see whether you can fill in the blanks with the missing forms of each word. Some may have the same spelling while others may not. One has been done for you.

Noun	Verb	Adjective	Adverb
perfection	to perfect	**perfect**	perfectly
agreement	_____	_____	_____
_____	_____	_____	**irritably**
_____	**to comfort**	_____	_____
_____	_____	**romantic**	_____

The Verb/Noun Shuffle

Some of the words in the following list are nouns, some of them are verbs, and some of them could be either. Your job is to shuffle the words into their correct spaces in the chart. Read carefully! There are five words for each column.

arise	delay	kindness	speak
cloud	eat	month	woman
color	face	icicle	write
danger	forgive	praise	

Verbs	Verbs or Nouns	Nouns

Transforming Words

As you've seen, some words function as only one part of speech, while other words easily function in multiple ways. What do you do if there is a word that you really want to use, but it isn't the correct part of speech? Don't worry. There are some suffixes, or word endings, that you can use to help transform your word into something you are able to use. Let's try a few out!

-OUS: This suffix means "full of" and can be used to transform words into adjectives. For example, if I was talking about a meat-eating dinosaur, I could say, "That carnivore is **carnivorous**." By adding the *-ous* ending, I was able to transform the noun "carnivore" into the adjective "carnivorous." You try a few, but be careful. Some of them aren't as easy as just adding an *-ous*:

1. ridicule (verb: to make fun of)

    _____ (adjective: absurd)

2. contagion (noun: a disease that can be transmitted)

    _____ (adjective: likely to spread and affect others)

3. scandal (noun: a disgraceful situation or damage to a reputation)

    _____ (adjective: disgraceful, shocking)

4. fame (noun: widespread and favorable reputation)

    _____ (adjective: renowned, celebrated)

5. cavern (noun: a cave, especially one that is large and mostly underground)

    _____ (adjective: deep-set, hollow, deep-sounding)

6. caution (noun: alertness in a hazardous situation; care)

    _____ (adjective: showing or using extra care)

7. grace (noun: favor or goodwill, elegance, or beauty)

    _____ (adjective: pleasantly kind, benevolent)

-TION: This suffix means "state or quality" and can be used to turn words into nouns. For example, if I **participated** in an event, I might talk about my **participation**. By adding the *-tion* ending to the verb, I turned it into a noun. You try a few, but be careful. Some of them aren't as easy as just adding a *-tion*:

8.   demonstrate (verb: to describe, explain, or illustrate by example)

    _____ (noun: something serving as proof or supporting evidence)

9.   elect (verb: to choose a leader by voting)

    _____ (noun: the selection of a person for office by voting)

10.   cite (verb: to quote OR to officially summon to court)

    _____ (noun: a summons to appear in court, a quote)

11.   extinct (adjective: no longer in existence, died out)

    _____ (noun: the act of dying out)

12.   alter (verb: to make different, to modify)

    _____ (noun: a change, modification, or adjustment)

13.   attentive (adjective: observant, thoughtful of others)

    _____ (noun: observant care, consideration)

14.   fascinating (adjective: of great interest, captivating)

    _____ (noun: powerful attraction, charm)

Context Cartoons

Carefully read the following cartoons and sentences. Based on the context clues provided, select the best definition for each of the bolded words.

1.

a) uncommonly talented
b) impossible to hear
c) mean-spirited teasing
d) famous

2. On the iPhone above, **predictive** text can be a useful
   feature, but it can also lead to amazing autocorrect
   fails. No matter how smart a phone is, it can't always
   know what you want to say before you say it.

   a) saying something will happen in the future
   b) abbreviated for efficiency
   c) grammatically incorrect
   d) inappropriate

Jon Le-Bon/Shutterstock.com

3. The former soldier was hired to **transport** cargo from one location to another with no questions asked, but the day he stopped to look in the trunk was the day things got crazy.

a) to work hard
b) to sell for profit
c) to fight tirelessly
d) to carry from one place to another

Korpithas/Shutterstock.com

4. When one is attempting to **construct** a home in a cave, the most important factor to consider is location. Building a home in a cave that is too wet, too remote, or has too many bats can only cause trouble.

a) demolish
b) find
c) build
d) dry out

ayelet-keshet/Shutterstock.com

5. While some people believe that **astrology** is nothing but hocus pocus, others think that studying the movements of the stars and planets is a valid way to make predictions about the future.

a) the study of how the stars and planets influence lives and behavior of people
b) the study of how the shape of the skull could indicate mental abilities and character
c) science that deals with the structure of substances and the changes that they go through
d) science concerned with how goods and services are produced, sold, and bought

The Pieces of the Puzzles

Many words are built with pieces that come from Latin and Greek words. The pieces fit together like puzzles to construct words. Although the word parts come from foreign languages you may have never studied, you probably know many of them already without realizing it. Based on the definitions of the words you just used in the previous section, see whether you can match the individual parts of each word to their definitions.

_____ 1. 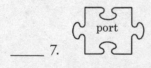 astro   a. across

_____ 2. aud   b. before

_____ 3. con   c. build

_____ 4. dict   d. hear

_____ 5. in   e. not

_____ 6. ology   f. star

_____ 7. port   g. study of

_____ 8. pre   h. to carry

_____ 9. struct   i. to say

_____ 10. trans   j. with

Putting Together the Puzzle

Read the following sentences. Based on the context clues and the definitions of the word parts, figure out which puzzle piece you need from the previous section to complete the word.

1. Although she normally felt just fine on airplanes, the _____ flight to France made her nervous. Knowing she was flying **across** the Atlantic Ocean made her very uncomfortable.

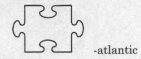
-atlantic

2. Caleb was confident when he went in for his _____. Even though it was going to be the first time someone other than his parents or his teacher would **hear** him play, he knew he was going to do a good job.

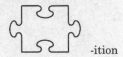
-ition

3. Ironman and Hulk were _____, working **with** each other in the same time and place to fight crime.

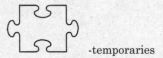
-temporaries

4. When Tomas was younger, he wanted to be an _____. He even sent away to **Space** Camp for a brochure when he was in sixth grade.

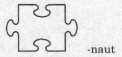
-naut

5. When Elizabeth decided that she wanted to **study** amphibians and reptiles, her friends in the _____ department playfully changed her name from Elizabeth to Lizard-breath.

herpet-
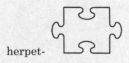

6. Although her tank top and shorts were perfect for the beach, they were **not** a good idea for the job interview. She didn't think an _____ outfit would help her to get the job.

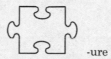 -appropriate

7. The company **built** an elaborate _____ in front of the corporate offices for the holidays, complete with decorations, lights, and animatronic animals.

 -ure

8. When countries trade with each other, they often buy and sell things like cars and oil. Sometimes, though, more unusual things are **carried** to other countries. Liechtenstein, for example, is the world's leading _____ of false teeth.

ex- 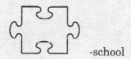 -er

9. Jasmine went to _____ when she was 4, before she went to kindergarten the next year.

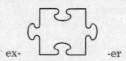 -school

10. Unfortunately, he has a _____ conversation style. Whenever you **say** something, he will argue the opposite.

contra- 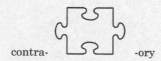 -ory

Expand It!

Can you think of any other words that use the following word parts? Feel free to use a dictionary to verify that the words you choose work with the word parts!

1. aud: _____

   _____

2. in: _____

   _____

3. astro: _____

   _____

4. ology: _____

   _____

5. con: _____

   _____

6. struct: _____

   _____

7. pre: _____

   _____

8. dict: _____

   _____

9. trans: _____

   _____

10. port: _____

    _____

Words in Context

You have seen one way to learn new words: learning the parts of the words and putting them together. That's a great way to increase your vocabulary, but it's impossible to learn every single vocabulary word you will ever need to know. So what do you do when you run into a word that you have never seen? The words around the unfamiliar word, called **context clues**, can help you figure out the meaning. Take a look at the following example:

> *I like flaumpens.*

Do you know what I like? Do you have any idea what I'm talking about? It could be just about anything. What if I said:

> *I like flaumpens, especially right out of the oven.*

Now you have more information! You still don't know what flaumpens is, but you probably feel fairly comfortable saying that it's something you cook and probably eat. Let's add a little more **context**.

> *I like flaumpens, especially right out of the oven. The combination of hot pastry and seasoned pork is just about the best taste ever.*

Now you know what flaumpens is! Even though I never actually gave you a definition, you can easily figure out that the word refers to a baked pastry with pork in it.

Find the Definition

Read each of the following sentences. Based on the information provided, see whether you can choose the best definition from the ones provided. Write the letter of the definition on the line beside the word. Not all definitions will be used.

1. When seawater mixes with fresh water, **brackish** _____ water is formed. Although it isn't as salty as seawater, its **salinity** _____ is too high for the water to be safe for drinking. In order to be **potable** _____, the brackish water must go through a **desalination** _____ process.

Masonjar/Shutterstock.com

   a) amount of salt in something
   b) removing salt
   c) seasoning with salt
   d) slightly salty
   e) suitable for drinking
   f) watering down

2. When Batman fights an **adversary** _____, his Bat-gadgets come in handy because he doesn't have any actual superpowers. His Bat-darts contain **tranquilizers** _____ that can knock out enemies and his Batarangs are a type of **shuriken** _____ that he can throw to cut things or hook things. These tools, in addition to many others, have earned Batman a reputation as one of the most **enterprising** _____ superheroes out there.

   a) criminal or inmate
   b) drugs that calm or induce sleep
   c) enemy or opponent
   d) Japanese decoration
   e) showing resourcefulness or creativity
   f) strong and fast
   g) weapon that is used for throwing

3. Hundreds of zombies **swarmed** _____ over the hillside, their **gaits** _____ awkward and stiff as they moved toward the town. The townspeople barricaded themselves in the Community Center, hoping their defense **tactics** _____ would be successful. Fortunately, the explosives that were **detonated** _____ near the edge of town took out a large number of the monsters.

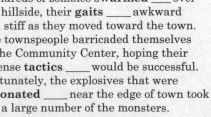

   a) carefully planned strategies
   b) moved somewhere in large numbers
   c) to block in or obstruct
   d) to creep slowly
   e) exploded with sudden violence
   f) ways of walking

Write the Definition

Read each of the following sentences. Underline the context clues that help you figure out the definition of the bolded word. Write your definition of the bolded word on the line provided. The first one has been done for you.

1. <u>Although</u> the boy used to be **boisterous** when he was in elementary and middle school, he <u>calmed down quite a bit</u> by the time he got to high school.

    <u>Rough and noisy</u>

2. Before Thomas Edison got the lightbulb to work, over ten thousand of his attempts were failures. Luckily, he stuck with the experiment, and because of his **tenacity**, we now have a way to see things at night-time.

    _____

3. Ebenezer Scrooge, the famous miser from Dickens' *A Christmas Carol*, is so **penurious** that he refuses to give even a little money to help the poor.

    _____

4. My goal of remaining **inconspicuous** was ruined when I tripped over my shoelace and crashed into a table, attracting the attention of everyone in the room.

    _____

5. The darkness of the countryside would have been almost complete if not for the **luminous** moon that helped light the path.

    _____

6. Rocks and sand grains frozen into glaciers can create glacial **striations** as the glacier moves, cutting parallel grooves in the bedrock below the ice.

    _____

Match the Definition

The following story is missing words. Read it carefully, and see whether you can match the words provided with the gaps in the story. Be sure to read the whole story—some of the context clues you need may not be immediately beside the missing words.

Marco went to the State Fair. He didn't care about the exhibits, the rides didn't excite him, and he didn't even look at the games. He was at the fair for one reason only: to eat. The choices were many, and the smells from the food tents rose into the air and mingled into a mouth-watering _____. His goal, as it was every

1
year, was to eat until he couldn't possibly eat anything else. He started slowly with roast corn and a caramel apple. Then he began to build up some _____

2
with fried vegetables, a giant turkey leg, and kettle corn. And that was just on the Midway. Later he found deep-fried candy bars, chicken-fried bacon, and corn dogs. He ventured into the exhibit halls, but only for the _____ of-

3
ferings. The cotton candy spun from pure maple sugar, the giant dill pickles, the hush puppy samples, and the homemade fudge. If he could find it, he ate it. The good, the bad, and the ugly. He was going strong for the first two hours, wandering the fairgrounds as he ate one snack after another. He was confident through the fresh-cut fries and barbecue, but began to _____ after

4
the ostrich burger. He plowed ahead, though—having been through the center of the fair, he still had to work his way around the _____ of the

5
fairgrounds to get back to his car. Nearly at his destination, he discovered a(n)
_____ he had never seen before. A normal hamburger, dressed

6
with cheese, lettuce, tomatoes, mustard, and ketchup, but instead of the regular sesame bun, the hamburger was served between two glazed doughnuts. It was the most _____ food item he had seen at the fair that year, and

7
would be the perfect way to end the trip. He took a bite and his stomach gave a(n)
_____ lurch. He took a deep breath, determined to finish it.

8
Four more bites, lots of careful chewing, and the burger was gone. And he was done until next year.

aroma (noun)	an odor arising from spices, plants, cooking, and so forth, especially an agreeable odor
circumference (noun)	the outer boundary, especially of a circular area; perimeter
concoction (noun)	a combination of ingredients
edible (adjective)	fit to be eaten as food
falter (verb)	to hesitate or waver
momentum (noun)	force or speed of movement
ominous (adjective)	threatening evil or harm
unique (adjective)	existing as the only one; not typical; unusual

Connotation versus Denotation

When someone asks you what a word means, what's the first thing you think of? Probably how the dictionary defines the word. That is the **denotation**, or "dictionary definition" of a word. We have been looking at the denotations of many words. That's not the only way to define a word, though. Consider the following sentences:

The slender teenager walked down the street.

The scrawny teenager walked down the street.

Those sentences are exactly the same, except for the words we used to describe the teenager. Both of those words, *slender* and *scrawny*, have a similar **denotation**: They both mean *thin*. However, having a similar meaning doesn't automatically mean they have a similar feeling. **Connotation** is the association connected to a word or the emotional suggestions a word brings. Words may have a positive connotation, a negative connotation, or a neutral connotation.

The kitchen was filled with the aroma of Jan's cooking.

The kitchen was filled with the stench of Donna's cooking.

Whose food would you rather eat? Probably Jan's? Why? Both *aroma* and *stench* mean *smell*. It's because you have an association with each of those words, and one is definitely positive while the other is strongly negative.

Connotations can help you figure out a general meaning of a word if you don't know the word or if you don't have enough context to figure out the exact meaning.

1. *I smiled and looked for the food when I walked into the house, which was redolent with the smell of Jamie's cooking.*

   Does Jamie's cooking smell good or bad? _____

   How do you know? _____

   Does *redolent* have a positive connotation or a negative connotation?

   _____

2. *I grimaced and pinched my nose when I walked into the house, which was noxious with the smell of Lee's cooking.*

   Does Lee's cooking smell good or bad? _____

   How do you know? _____

   Does *noxious* have a positive connotation or a negative connotation?

   _____

Create the Mood

The following sentences are neutral sentences. Your job is to rewrite the sentences to give the subjects more favorable or unfavorable connotations.

1. *The flight attendant brought drinks to the travelers and handed a blanket to a lady with a baby.*

    Rewrite this sentence so the trip is a pleasant experience.

    _____

    _____

    _____

    Rewrite this sentence so the trip is an unpleasant experience.

    _____

    _____

    _____

2. *The crowd gathered outside the building with their signs.*

    Rewrite this sentence so the gathering crowd is a good thing.

    _____

    _____

    _____

    Rewrite this sentence so the gathering crowd is a bad thing.

    _____

    _____

    _____

ANSWERS

Functions of Words

1. jail; noun (a place)
2. baby; verb (an action)
3. baby; adjective (describing "panda")
4. work; adjective (describing "day")
5. word; verb (an action)
6. work; verb (an action)
7. jail; verb (an action)
8. word; noun (a thing)
9. baby; noun (a person)
10. word; adjective (describing "games")

Description Conniption

The day of the (costume) contest had [finally] arrived. Mrs. Fuzzypaws woke with butterflies in her stomach. Or maybe that was just a hairball. No matter. Today was the day! She could feel it. This year was going to be her year. Tibsy had taken Grand Champion the [past] (two) years, first for her [outrageously] (clever) Catopatra outfit and then (last) year with her Queen Feline getup. Mrs. Fuzzypaws knew that (second) place was nothing to sneeze at, but she [desperately] wanted to win. And (this) year, she figured it was in the bag. Relevant, [well]-made, and clever, the (scarlet) and gold scarf had been knitted [precisely] to fit her neck, and the wig had [carefully] been curled and then frizzed. A (quick) lick of the paws, a clip of the nails, and she was ready to make her debut … as Purr-mione Granger.

Bring It All Together!

Noun	Verb	Adjective	Adverb
perfection	to perfect	**perfect**	perfectly
agreement	to agree	agreeable	agreeably
irritant	to irritate	irritable	**irritably**
comfort	**to comfort**	comfortable	comfortably
romance	to romance	**romantic**	romantically

The Verb/Noun Shuffle

Verbs	Verbs or Nouns	Nouns
arise	face	icicle
eat	cloud	kindness
forgive	color	month
speak	delay	woman
write	praise	danger

Transforming Words

-OUS

1. ridiculous
2. contagious
3. scandalous
4. famous
5. cavernous
6. cautious
7. gracious

-TION

8. demonstration
9. election
10. citation
11. extinction
12. alteration
13. attention
14. fascination

Context Cartoons

1. b
2. a
3. d
4. c
5. a

The Pieces of the Puzzle

1. f
2. d
3. j
4. i
5. e
6. g
7. h
8. b
9. c
10. a

Putting Together the Puzzle

1. **trans**-atlantic
2. **aud**-ition
3. **con**-temporaries
4. **astro**-naut
5. herpet-**ology**
6. **in**-appropriate
7. **struct**-ure
8. ex-**port**-er
9. **pre**-school
10. contra-**dict**-ory

Expand It! (answers may vary)

1. audience, auditorium, auditory
2. ineligible, inaccurate, incorrect
3. astrodome, astronomer, asteroid
4. biology, oncology, etymology, zoology
5. concur, convention, contact
6. instruct, destruction, deconstruct
7. prepare, preamble, prehistoric
8. diction, dictator, benediction
9. transfer, transformer, transfusion
10. portable, porter, support, deport

Find the Definition
1. d, a, e, b
2. c, b, g, e
3. b, f, a, e

Write the Definition (definitions may vary)
2. Before Thomas Edison got the lightbulb to work, over ten thousand of his attempts were failures. Luckily, <u>he stuck with the experiment</u>, and because of his tenacity, we now have a way to see things at night-time. *sticking to something*

3. Ebenezer Scrooge, the famous <u>miser</u> from Dickens' *A Christmas Carol*, is so penurious that he <u>refuses to give even a little money</u> to help the poor. *stingy, penny-pinching*

4. My goal of remaining inconspicuous was <u>ruined</u> when I tripped over my shoelace and crashed into a table, <u>attracting the attention of everyone</u> in the room. *unnoticed*

5. The darkness of the countryside would have been almost complete if not for the luminous moon that helped <u>light the path</u>. *giving off light*

6. Rocks and sand grains frozen into glaciers can create glacial striations as the glacier moves, <u>cutting parallel grooves</u> in the bedrock below the ice. *lines, marks, grooves*

Match the Definition
1. aroma
2. momentum
3. edible
4. falter
5. circumference
6. concoction
7. unique
8. ominous

Connotation versus Denotation
1. good; "I smiled and looked for the food"; positive
2. bad; "I grimaced and pinched my nose"; negative

Create the Mood (answers may vary)

1. The helpful flight attendant brought cold drinks to the thirsty travelers and handed a soft blanket to a grateful lady with a sleepy baby.

   The cranky flight attendant brought expensive drinks to the miserable travelers and handed a scratchy blanket to a tired lady with a screaming baby.

2. The excited crowd gathered noisily outside the performance building with their fan signs.

   The angry crowd gathered ominously outside the government building with their protest signs.

Purpose and Point of View

Author: Lisa Mayo

PURPOSE AND POINT OF VIEW

Understanding a book, a poem, or even a text message often requires more than simply knowing *what* an author says. Frequently, recognizing *why* an author makes a particular statement is equally necessary to grasping his or her main point. Additionally, many reading comprehension questions on standardized tests, such as the SAT or ACT, ask for the purpose of specific words, sentences, and paragraphs. Therefore, discovering the different reasons why authors write, and learning how to identify those reasons, is crucial.

Purposes of Sentences

When authors write, they do so for many of the same reasons that you write: to provide information, to make people laugh, to convey emotion, or to convince others of a certain argument, among other things. Putting yourself in the place of an author, and thinking about the reasons why you might write similar statements can help you to discover an author's purpose. Consider the statement below.

> *Grit in a sensitive instrument, or a crack in one of his own high-power lenses, would not be more disturbing than a strong emotion in a nature such as his.*

To discover the writer's purpose, ask yourself two questions.

1. *What* does the author say?
2. *Why* does he or she make that statement?

In this case, *what* the author says is that the man in question would be disturbed if he felt strong emotions. Now examine *why* the author makes this statement. The sentence describes the way that a particular man reacts to emotion. Why might you explain how someone reacts to a particular thing? You would probably do so to provide a picture of that person's character. Therefore, the purpose of this sentence is likely to give you, as the reader, a better understanding of the man's character.

Read the sentence below, and use the questions that follow to help you identify the purpose of the sentence.

> *Far away on the path we saw Sir Henry looking back, his face white in the moonlight, his hands raised in horror, glaring helplessly at the frightful thing which was hunting him down.*

1. *What* does the author say?

_____

_____

2. *Why* does he or she make that statement?

_____

_____

Here, *what* the author states is that Sir Henry looked pale, that his hands were raised in horror, and that something fearful was hunting him. *Why* does the author give you this information? The situation that the author describes is somewhat scary, so the author is likely attempting to build suspense and to convey just how terrifying the event was.

Read the sentence below, and use the questions that follow to identify the purpose of the sentence.

> *Consider Edgar Allan Poe's "The Purloined Letter," which cannot truly be considered a mystery story because Poe identifies the thief at the outset.*

1. *What* does the author say?

_____

_____

2. *Why* does he or she make that statement?

_____

_____

In the sentence above, *what* the author states is that "The Purloined Letter" cannot be considered a mystery because readers know from the beginning who committed the crime. *Why* does the author make that statement? Notice that the author uses the word "consider" to begin the sentence. Why might you use the word "consider" to begin a sentence? You would probably use it to introduce an example. In this case, therefore, the author is likely introducing an example of a story that is not a genuine mystery.

Read the sentence below, and use the questions that follow to identify the purpose of the sentence.

> *At first glance, the question may appear unnecessary and the answer quite obvious.*

1. *What* does the author say?

_____

_____

2.   *Why* does he or she make that statement?

_____

_____

In this sentence, *what* the author states is that the question may seem redundant, and that the answer to the question might seem obvious. *Why* does the author make this statement? Notice that the sentence begins with the phrase *at first glance*. Why might you use that phrase? Often, people use the phrase *at first glance* to suggest that a deeper, more thorough look will provide a different point of view. Hence, in this case, the author must be writing to show that the question only outwardly appears to have an obvious answer, and that a more careful look will show that the question is not unnecessary and that the answer is not obvious.

The Purposes of Sentences in Paragraphs

As you can see, sometimes one or two words can determine the purpose of an entire sentence. Therefore, reading closely and paying attention to the specific wording that authors use is vital to understanding their purposes in writing. At other times, however, looking merely at the words within a sentence may not be enough; you may need to look at the surrounding sentences in order to gain a greater understanding of the context before you can identify the purpose of a thought. Consider the paragraph below.

> *Who really was responsible for the murder of James Gatz, or as he later became known to the world, Jay Gatsby? In his novel <u>The Great Gatsby</u>, F. Scott Fitzgerald plainly tells the story of how George Wilson shot and killed Gatsby in mid-afternoon on a summer's day. However, stating that Wilson killed Gatsby is really only a superficial answer to the question. Wilson may have been the tool that delivered death to Gatsby, but the forces that brought that tool to Gatsby were many and subtle. Greed, misguided idealism, and selfishness all contributed their parts, operating for years behind the scenes to create the final event of Gatsby's death.*

What is the purpose of the sentence below?

> *Greed, misguided idealism, and selfishness all contributed their parts, operating for years behind the scenes to create the final event of Gatsby's death.*

1.   *What* does the author say?

The author indicates that greed, misguided idealism, and selfishness all helped to cause Gatsby's death.

2.   *Why* does she make that statement?

In order to understand *why* the author says this, it's important to consider what she was discussing immediately before this statement. Consider this earlier sentence.

However, stating that Wilson killed Gatsby is really only a superficial answer to the question.

Here, the author claims that blaming Wilson for Gatsby's death doesn't truly explain Gatsby's death. After that she goes on to mention three things—greed, misguided idealism, and selfishness—that also helped to cause Gatsby's death. Why does she mention these things, then? The answer must be that she mentions them to support her earlier claim that blaming Wilson for Gatsby's death doesn't truly explain Gatsby's death.

When you are looking for the purpose of a particular sentence within a passage, remember: The sentence doesn't exist in a vacuum. The sentences that come immediately before and immediately after will discuss related ideas. Your job as the reader is to connect those ideas so that you can see how they relate to one another. Once you understand this relationship, you'll understand the purpose of each sentence.

Now see whether you can identify the purpose of a particular sentence on your own. Consider the paragraph below.

The most essential thing in the world for any individual is to understand himself. The next is to understand the other fellow. The truth is that life is largely a problem of running your own car as it was built to be run, and then of getting along with the other drivers on the highway. We come in contact with our fellowmen in all the activities of our lives and what we get out of life depends, to an astounding degree, on our relations with them.

Examine the sentence below, and use the questions that follow to identify the purpose of the sentence. Write your answers in the blank spaces below each question.

The truth is that life is largely a problem of running your own car as it was built to be run, and then of getting along with the other drivers on the highway.

1.   *What* does the author say?

_____

_____

2.   What does the author discuss immediately before this sentence?

      _____

      _____

3.   What does the author discuss immediately after this sentence?

      _____

      _____

4.   Consider how these thoughts fit together. *Why* does he or she make
      that statement?

      _____

      _____

In this case, *what* the author says is that one of the most important issues in life is running your car in the way that it was meant to be run, and that one of the other important issues in life is getting along with other drivers.

Why does the author say this? Consider the two sentences that appear immediately before this sentence. In these sentences, the author discusses how important it is for each of us to understand ourselves, and how important it is for us to understand our neighbors. Now consider the sentence that appears at the end of the paragraph. That sentence states that what we get out of life depends on our relations with other people.

How do these sentences relate to the sentence in question? Since the rest of the paragraph focuses on the importance of understanding ourselves and others, the sentence in question must also be related to the importance of understanding ourselves and others. Therefore, *running your own car* must relate to the idea of understanding yourself, and *getting along with other drivers* must relate to understanding and getting along with others in life. Thus, the author is illustrating her idea by using a metaphor in which she compares driving to life. So the purpose of the sentence must be to provide an illustration of the author's previous two sentences.

See whether you can identify the purpose of a particular phrase on your own. Consider the paragraph below.

> I am a very old man; how old I do not know. Possibly I am a hundred, possibly more; but I cannot tell because I have never aged as other men, nor do I remember any childhood. So far as I can recollect I have always been a man, a man of about thirty. I appear today as I did forty years and more ago, and yet I feel that I cannot go on living forever; that someday I shall die the real death from which there is no resurrection. I do not know why I should fear death, I who have died twice and am still alive; but yet I have the same horror of it as you who have never died, and it is because of this terror of death, I believe, that I am so convinced of my mortality.

Examine the phrase below and use the questions that follow to identify the purpose of the phrase. Write your answers in the blank spaces below each question.

> So far as I can recollect…

1. *What* does the author say?

    _____

    _____

2. What does the author discuss immediately before this sentence?

    _____

    _____

3. What does the author discuss immediately after this sentence?

    _____

    _____

4. Consider how these thoughts fit together. What is the purpose of the phrase in question?

    _____

    _____

Here, *what* the narrator essentially says is that the information he is giving is true *as far as he knows*. *Why* does he say that? Examine the sentences that appear before this phrase. In these sentences he states that he does not know how old he is, and that he might be one hundred years old, but that he cannot tell for sure. Now examine the sentence that appears after that phrase. In that sentence, he states that he appears the same today as he did forty years ago. Both the sentences that appear immediately before and immediately after the phrase in question discuss the idea that the author does not seem to have aged, and he is not certain how old he really is. Therefore, this phrase must also relate to this idea. The purpose of the phrase is to demonstrate that the narrator might be wrong; he is not actually certain how old he is.

Read the paragraph below, and answer the questions that follow.

> *I shall read your book with trembling for you. Some years ago, when you were beginning to tell me your real name and birthplace, you may remember I stopped you, and preferred to remain ignorant of all. So I continued until the other day, when you read me your memoirs. I hardly knew, at the time, whether to thank you or not for the sight of them, when I reflected that it was still dangerous, in Massachusetts, for honest men to tell their names! They say the fathers, in 1776, signed the Declaration of Independence with the noose practically about their necks. You, too, publish your declaration of freedom with danger surrounding you on all sides. In all the broad lands which the Constitution of the United States overshadows, there is no single spot,—however narrow or desolate,—where a fugitive slave can plant himself and say, "I am safe."*

Examine the sentence below and use the questions that follow to identify the purpose of the sentence. Write your answers in the blank spaces below each question.

> *They say the fathers, in 1776, signed the Declaration of Independence with the noose practically about their necks.*

1. *What* does the author say?

   _____

   _____

2. What does the author discuss immediately before this sentence?

   _____

   _____

3. What does the author discuss immediately after this sentence?

   _____

   _____

4. Consider how these thoughts fit together. *Why* did he or she write the sentence in question?

_____

_____

What the author says is that when the country's founding fathers signed the Declaration of Independence, they practically had nooses around their necks. Because a noose is used for hanging, the author must be saying that the founding fathers were in danger. Now consider what the author says immediately before the sentence in question. He states that it was dangerous for men in Massachusetts to reveal their names. Now consider what he says immediately after the sentence in question. Here, he states that the man to whom he is talking is surrounded by danger. So how do these thoughts fit together? The author discusses the fact that the man to whom is he speaking is in danger, and then discusses another instance of people who were in danger. Therefore, he must be using the sentence *They say the fathers, in 1776, signed the Declaration of Independence with the noose practically about their necks* to provide an example of a similar situation in which people were in danger.

Are You Ready for the SAT and ACT?

If you're taking a standardized test such as the SAT or the ACT, you are likely to see a number of reading comprehension questions that ask you about the purposes of specific phrases or sentences. To answer these questions, begin by using the same process that you've used to answer questions earlier in this chapter. First, consider what the author says in the phrase or sentence in question. Then, look at what the author says immediately before and immediately after the phrase or sentence in question. Finally, think about how these thoughts connect, and see whether you can explain, in your own words, why the author writes what he or she does. Wait until you have that answer before you go to the answer choices. If you know what you're looking for, you'll be much more likely to recognize the correct answer when you see it.

Ready to put your reading skills to use in a standardized test-style question? Read the paragraph below, and answer the multiple-choice question that follows.

> I had neither kith nor kin in England, and was therefore as free as air—or as free as an income of eleven shillings and sixpence a day will permit a man to be. Under such circumstances, I naturally gravitated to London, that great cesspool into which all the loungers and idlers of the Empire are irresistibly drained. There I stayed for some time at a private hotel in the Strand, leading a comfortless, meaningless existence, and spending such money as I had, considerably more freely than I ought. So alarming did the state of my finances become, that I soon realized that I must either leave the metropolis and rusticate somewhere in the country, or that I must make a complete alteration in my style of living. Choosing the latter alternative, I began by making up my mind to leave the hotel, and to take up my quarters in some less pretentious and less expensive domicile.

1. The primary purpose of the phrase *as free as an income of eleven shillings and sixpence a day will permit a man to be* is to

   a) indicate that the narrator's wealth contributed to his freedom
   b) explain why the narrator preferred to live in London
   c) qualify a statement that the narrator made earlier in the paragraph
   d) support the claim that the narrator would never experience true liberty
   e) imply that the narrator would inevitably become homeless

What helps identify the primary purpose of the phrase? Consider first *what* the author says. He indicates that he has as much freedom as he can get from an income of eleven shillings and six pence per day. What does he discuss immediately before this sentence? He mentions that he is *as free as air*. What does he discuss after this sentence? He tells you that he went to London, where he spent money more freely than he should have, and that he needed to either move to the country or change his way of life. Thus, he must not truly be *as free as air*, so the phrase in question qualifies, or limits that statement; the narrator is really only as free as his income will allow him to be. Therefore, the correct answer is choice (c). Because the narrator indicates that he has been spending more money than he should, and needs to move, his income limits, rather than contributes to his freedom, so choice (a) is not the credited answer. The narrator does mention that he gravitated toward London, but the phrase in question does not explain why he gravitated toward London, so choice (b) is incorrect. Choice (d) is too extreme; the narrator's freedom may be limited right now, but nothing in the text indicates that he will never be truly free. Choice (e) is similarly too extreme, because while the narrator says that he needs to change his lifestyle, he does not say that he cannot avoid becoming homeless.

Purposes of Paragraphs

Sometimes understanding a passage requires understanding not just the purpose of a particular sentence, but rather the purpose of an entire paragraph. To find the purpose of a paragraph, ask yourself the following questions:

1. What is the main topic of the paragraph?
2. *What* does the author say about that topic?
3. *Why* does the author write about that topic?

Consider the paragraph below.

> *Of all egotists, Montaigne, if not the greatest, was the most fascinating, because, perhaps, he was the least affected and most truthful. What he did, and what he had professed to do, was to dissect his mind, and show us, as best he could, how it was made, and what relation it bore to external objects. He investigated his mental structure as a schoolboy pulls his watch to pieces, to examine the mechanism of the works; and the result, accompanied by illustrations abounding with originality and force, he delivered to his fellow-men in a book.*

1. What is the main topic of the paragraph?

   The main topic of the paragraph is Montaigne, an egotist.

2. *What* does the author say about this topic?

   The author says that Montaigne was the most fascinating egotist because he was the not affected and he was truthful. Montaigne tried to explain how his mind worked.

3. *Why* does the author write about the topic?

   Note what the author does: He explains that Montaigne was great, and then give reasons why Montaigne was great. Thus, the purpose of the paragraph must be to explain why Montaigne was great, and to convince you that Montaigne was great.

Recycled Purposes

Finding the purpose of a paragraph can be tricky! Fortunately, however, authors don't invent a new purpose for every new paragraph they write. There are some purposes that you could think of as "popular" purposes because authors use them frequently. What are these purposes?

1. **To provide a description or present information.**

   Authors may describe people, places, events, things, or ideas, or may just give you information about those people or things. If you're reading a paragraph that seems as though it is merely a collection of facts, then you may be reading a paragraph that was written to inform or describe. Here's an example of a paragraph that was written to describe a person.

   This black-eyed, wide-mouthed girl, not pretty but full of life—with black curls tossed backward, thin, bare arms, little legs in lace-frilled drawers, and feet in low slippers—was just at that charming age when a girl is no longer a child, though the child is not yet a young woman. Escaping from her father she ran to hide her flushed face in the lace of her mother's shawl—not paying the least attention to her severe remark— and began to laugh. She laughed, and in fragmentary sentences tried to explain about a doll which she produced from the folds of her frock.

   The main topic of this paragraph is the girl; the author explains that she is not pretty, but she is full of life. So, *why* does the author write this paragraph? The author's purpose in writing the paragraph is to describe the girl.

2. **To contradict another point of view.**

   Sometimes authors write simply to prove that someone else's point of view is incorrect. Here is a paragraph written to contradict another point of view.

   Certain authors, following Varro, have maintained that the civilization of Rome died a "natural death," the normal result of old age. It is mere fancy to suppose that nations have their birth, their maturity, and their decline under an unbreakable law like that which determines the life history of the individual. A nation may be broken up if wrongly led or attacked by a superior force, and it will suffer if its population of effective leaders is reduced. Such effects, rather than those of nature, caused the decline of Rome.

   The main topic of this paragraph is the decline of Rome; the author says that it is *mere fancy*, or wrong, to assume that Rome died as a result of natural decay. He then goes on to list the items that he believes caused the fall of Rome. So *why* did the author write this paragraph? He must have written it to contradict the point of view that Rome died as *the normal result of old age.*

3. **To make an argument.**

Often, authors write to convince others to accept their points of view. They may argue for an idea, for a solution to a problem, or for a particular course of action. If you think that you are reading a paragraph that is designed to make an argument, ask yourself, "what does the author want me to believe about this topic?" If you find that you can point to a specific idea with which the author wants you to agree, you are probably reading a paragraph that was written to argue a point. Examine the paragraph below and see whether you can identify the author's argument.

There is probably one purpose, and only one, for which the use of force by a government is beneficial, and that is to diminish the total amount of force used by others in the world. It is clear, for example, that the legal prohibition of murder diminishes the total amount of violence in the world. So long as some men wish to do violence to others, there cannot be complete liberty, for either the wish to do violence must be restrained, or the victims must be left to suffer. For this reason, although individuals and societies should have the utmost freedom as regards their own lives, they ought not to have complete freedom as regards their dealings with others. To give freedom to the strong to oppress the weak is not the way to secure the greatest possible amount of freedom in the world.

The main topic of the paragraph is the use of force by governments. The author states that this force is beneficial only when it limits the total amount of force in the world, and that unless people's freedoms are limited to some extent, then the strong will be able to oppress the weak. *Why* did the author write this paragraph, then? It must have been to convince readers that governments must sometimes use force to limit the freedoms of their citizens.

4. **To explore or examine ideas.**

Authors write some paragraphs because they simply want to discuss new ideas. They may want to point out that a particular problem does not yet have a solution or that there are multiple possible answers to a question. Here's an example of a paragraph that was written to explore a new idea.

Stereotypes and preconceptions abound about Generation Y, often defined as the generation of individuals born on or after 1982. Some predict that this generation will be more civic-minded than its predecessors, possessing a strong sense of community. Others, however, point to the current tendency of Generation Y members to immerse themselves in technology as evidence that this generation may, in fact, be less civic-minded. Such ones argue that teenagers who never seem to remove ear buds from their ears and who prefer texting and instant messaging to face-to-face speech are less likely to develop personal ties with others and are therefore less likely to have strong connections to their local communities as they grow older. Which side is correct? The truth is that only time will tell.

What is the topic of the paragraph? The author focuses on the stereotypes about Generation Y. She explores two different points of view about the generation, and then states that right now, no one can determine which side is correct. *Why* did the author write this paragraph, then? She must have written it in order to explore different stereotypes regarding Generation Y.

5. **To provide an explanation.**

Authors don't just make statements; they also explain why those statements are true. Often, they'll use entire paragraphs to explain a particular point of view, event, or thing. Check out the paragraph below, which provides an explanation for a particular phenomenon. As you read, see whether you can identify what the author is explaining.

He was so badly dressed that even a man accustomed to shabbiness would have been ashamed to be seen in the street in such rags. In that quarter of the town, however, scarcely any shortcoming in dress would have created surprise. Owing to the proximity of the market, the number of establishments of bad character, the abundance of the trading and working class population crowded in these streets and alleys in the heart of Petersburg, types so various were to be seen in the streets that no figure, however bizarre, would have caused surprise.

The topic of the paragraph is the shabbiness of the man's clothes, and of the town surrounding the man. What the author says about this topic is that no one was surprised by the shabbiness of the man's clothing because everyone in the area was accustomed to seeing people who were badly dressed. *Why* did the author write this paragraph, then? He must have written it in order to explain why no one was surprised by the shabbiness of the man's clothing.

Of course, not all paragraphs will fit into one of these five categories, and some paragraphs may fit into more than one category. However, if you are having trouble identifying the purpose of a paragraph, you may find it helpful to consider whether you can place the paragraph under one of these headings.

Now try a few paragraphs on your own. Answer the questions that follow each paragraph, and look for common purposes.

For many years various European collections of Egyptian antiquities have contained a certain series of objects which gave archaeologists great difficulty. There were vases of a peculiar form and color, greenish plates of slate, many of them in curious animal forms, and other similar things. It was known, positively, that these objects had been found in Egypt, but it was impossible to assign them a place in the known periods of Egyptian art. The puzzle was increased in difficulty by certain plates of slate with hunting and battle scenes and other representations in relief in a style so strange that many investigators considered them products of the art of Western Asia.

1. What is the main topic of the paragraph?

    _____

    _____

2. *What* does the author say about that topic?

    _____

    _____

3. *Why* does the author write about that topic?

    _____

    _____

The main topic of this paragraph is a collection of Egyptian antiquities. *What* the author says is that the collection contained peculiar items and that it was impossible to determine the period in which they had been created. *Why* did the author write this paragraph? The author just provides information about the puzzle surrounding the collection, so his purpose must have been to describe the puzzle surrounding the antiquities.

Examine the paragraph below, and answer the questions that follow.

It was at the post office that, several years ago, I saw Ethan Frome for the first time, and the sight pulled me up sharp. Even then he was the most striking figure in Starkfield, though he was but the ruin of a man. It was not so much his great height that marked him, for the "natives" were easily singled out by their lank longitude from the stockier foreign breed: it was the careless powerful look he had, in spite of a lameness checking each step like the jerk of a chain. There was something bleak and unapproachable in his face, and he was so stiffened and grizzled that I took him for an old man and was surprised to hear that he was not more than fifty-two. I had this from Harmon Gow, who had driven the stage from Bettsbridge to Starkfield in pre-trolley days and knew the chronicle of all the families on his line.

1.   What is the main topic of the paragraph?

2.   *What* does the author say about that topic?

3.   *Why* does the author write about that topic?

The topic of the paragraph is Ethan Frome. *What* the author says is that Ethan was the most striking figure in town. She then proceeds to give details about how Ethan was striking. *Why* did the author write the paragraph? The purpose of this paragraph must be to explain why Ethan Frome was striking.

Purposes of Paragraphs Within Passages

In some cases, you may need to find the purpose that a particular paragraph serves within an entire passage. In order to find that purpose, you'll want to examine both what comes before and what comes after, just as you would if you were finding the purpose of a sentence within a paragraph. Consider the passage below.

> *On March 5, 1867, the Moravian from the Montreal Ocean Company, ran its starboard quarter afoul of a rock marked on no charts of these waterways. Under the combined efforts of wind and 400-horsepower steam, it was traveling at a speed of thirteen knots. Without the high quality of its hull, the Moravian would surely have split open from this collision and gone down together with those 237 passengers it was bringing back from Canada.*

> *This accident happened around five o'clock in the morning, just as day was beginning to break. The officers on watch rushed to the craft's stern. They examined the ocean with the most scrupulous care. They saw nothing except a strong eddy breaking three cable lengths out, as if those sheets of water had been violently churned. The site's exact bearings were taken, and the Moravian continued on course apparently undamaged. Had it run afoul of an underwater rock or the wreckage of some enormous derelict ship? They were unable to say. But when they examined its undersides in the service yard, they discovered that part of its keel had been smashed.*

This occurrence, extremely serious in itself, might perhaps have been forgotten like so many others, if three weeks later it hadn't been reenacted under identical conditions. Only, thanks to the nationality of the ship victimized by this new ramming, and thanks to the reputation of the company to which this ship belonged, the event caused an immense uproar.

No one is unaware of the name of that famous English ship owner, Cunard. In 1840 this shrewd industrialist founded a postal service between Liverpool and Halifax, featuring three wooden ships with 400-horsepower paddle wheels and a burden of 1,162 metric tons. Eight years later, the company's assets were increased by four 650-horsepower ships at 1,820 metric tons, and in two more years, by two other vessels of still greater power and tonnage. In 1853 the Cunard Co., whose mail-carrying charter had just been renewed, successively added to its assets the Arabia, the Persia, the China, the Scotia, the Java, and the Russia, all ships of top speed and, after the Great Eastern, the biggest ever to plow the seas. So in 1867 this company owned twelve ships, eight with paddle wheels and four with propellers.

No transoceanic navigational undertaking has been conducted with more ability, no business dealings have been crowned with greater success. Given this, no one will be astonished at the uproar provoked by this accident involving one of its finest steamers.

Can you identify the purpose of the fourth paragraph in the passage? Use the questions below to find that purpose.

1. What is the main topic of the fourth paragraph?

    _____

    _____

2. *What* does the author say about that topic?

    _____

    _____

3. *What* does the author discuss in the paragraph immediately before this paragraph?

    _____

    _____

4. What does the author discuss in the paragraph immediately following this paragraph?

    _____

    _____

5. Consider how these thoughts relate to one another. *Why* did the author write the fourth paragraph?

    _____

    _____

The topic of the fourth paragraph is the Cunard Company. *What* does the author say about this company? He says that it is famous; it has large, powerful ships, and assets all over the world. In the paragraph immediately before the fourth paragraph, the author states that because of the company involved in the second accident, that accident caused an enormous uproar. In the paragraph immediately following the fourth paragraph, the author again emphasizes that the Cunard Company was successful, which is why no one was surprised that the Cunard ship's accident caused such an uproar. So, *why* did the author write the fourth paragraph? He must have written it to provide evidence to explain why the company was important and to explain why the ship's crash caused such concern. Without the fourth paragraph, you would not know why the Cunard Company was so important.

Notice that in the preceding example, you might not have been able to find the purpose of the fourth paragraph if you had not read the paragraphs immediately before and immediately after the fourth paragraph. Understanding context is important!

SAT Questions and the Purposes of Paragraphs
On the SAT and other standardized tests, you are likely to see a number of questions that ask you to find the purposes of paragraphs. Now that you know how to find the purposes of paragraphs, take a look at the question below to see how the SAT might test this topic.

It is with a kind of fear that I begin to write the history of my life. I have, as it were, a superstitious hesitation in lifting the veil that clings about my childhood like a golden mist. The task of writing an autobiography is a difficult one. When I try to classify my earliest impressions, I find that fact and fancy look alike across the years that link the past with the present. The woman paints the child's experiences in her own fantasy. A few impressions stand out vividly from the first years of my life; but "the shadows of the prison-house are on the rest." Besides, many of the joys and sorrows of childhood have lost their poignancy; and many incidents of vital importance in my early education have been forgotten in the excitement of great discoveries. Therefore, I find that I am only able to present a series of sketches of the episodes that seem to me to be the most interesting and important.

8. The primary purpose of the passage is to

   a) catalogue a set of impressions
   b) describe an important event
   c) criticize a point of view
   d) explain a difficulty
   e) defend a superstition

How did you answer this question? To find the correct answer, first consider the main topic of the paragraph: the author's task of writing an autobiography. *What* does the author say about that task? She says that she is nervous about writing her autobiography because the task will be difficult, and then she goes on to state why it will be difficult. Therefore, you could say that the purpose of the paragraph is to explain why the author believes that writing an autobiography will be difficult. Now examine your answers, and eliminate those that do not agree with the primary purpose of the paragraph. Because the paragraph discusses not only the author's impressions but also focuses on why those impressions make her task difficult, choice (a) is not the credited answer. No events are described within the paragraph, so you can eliminate choice (b). The author does not criticize any ideas, so choice (c) is incorrect. The author does explain why writing an autobiography will be difficult, so choice (d) agrees with the primary purpose of the paragraph. Finally, while the author does mention that she has an almost superstitious fear of examining her childhood, she does not defend that superstition. Thus, the correct answer is choice (d).

Finding the Big Picture: Purposes of Passages

Once you understand how to find the purposes of individual sentences and paragraphs, you can apply those same skills to finding the primary purposes of whole passages. To find the purpose of a passage, ask yourself the following questions:

1. What is the main topic of the passage?
2. *What* does the author say about that topic?
3. *Why* does the author write about that topic?

When you look for the topic of the passage, consider: What is the main subject of the passage? In other words, on what person or thing is the passage focusing? Then consider what you know about that person or thing from the passage. The answer to the third question above will provide you with the primary purpose of the passage. If you're having trouble finding the main idea of a passage as a whole, consider each of the paragraphs within that passage separately, and try to determine the purpose of each one. Then once you have the purpose of each paragraph, consider the paragraphs as a group to see whether you can find the overall purpose of the passage.

Ready to tackle a whole passage? Check out the excerpt below from H.G. Wells' novel *The Time Traveler,* and use the questions that follow to help you determine the purpose of the passage.

> 'This little affair,' said the Time Traveler, resting his elbows upon the table and pressing his hands together above the apparatus, 'is only a model. It is my plan for a machine to travel through time. You will notice that it looks singularly askew, and that there is an odd twinkling appearance about this bar, as though it was in some way unreal.' He pointed to the part with his finger. 'Also, here is one little white lever, and here is another.'

> The Medical Man got up out of his chair and peered into the thing. 'It's beautifully made,' he said.

> 'It took two years to make,' retorted the Time Traveler. Then, when we had all imitated the action of the Medical Man, he said: 'Now I want you clearly to understand that this lever, being pressed over, sends the machine gliding into the future, and this other reverses the motion. This saddle represents the seat of a time traveler. Presently I am going to press the lever, and off the machine will go. It will vanish, pass into future Time, and disappear. Have a good look at the thing. Look at the table too, and satisfy yourselves there is no trickery. I don't want to waste this model, and then be told I'm a quack.'

> There was a minute's pause perhaps. The Psychologist seemed about to speak to me, but changed his mind. Then the Time Traveler put forth his finger towards the lever. 'No,' he said suddenly. 'Lend me your hand.' And turning to the Psychologist, he took that individual's

hand in his own and told him to put out his forefinger. So that it was the Psychologist himself who sent forth the model Time Machine on its interminable voyage. We all saw the lever turn. I am absolutely certain there was no trickery. There was a breath of wind, and the lamp flame jumped. One of the candles on the mantel was blown out, and the little machine suddenly swung round, became indistinct, was seen as a ghost for a second perhaps, as an eddy of faintly glittering brass and ivory; and it was gone—vanished! Save for the lamp the table was bare.

Everyone was silent for a minute. Then Filby said he was astonished.

The Psychologist recovered from his stupor, and suddenly looked under the table. At that the Time Traveler laughed cheerfully. 'Well?' he said, with a reminiscence of the Psychologist. Then, getting up, he went to the tobacco jar on the mantel, and with his back to us began to fill his pipe.

We stared at each other. 'Look here,' said the Medical Man, 'are you in earnest about this? Do you seriously believe that that machine has travelled into time?'

'Certainly,' said the Time Traveler, stooping to light a spill at the fire. Then he turned, lighting his pipe, to look at the Psychologist's face. (The Psychologist, to show that he was not unhinged, helped himself to a cigar and tried to light it uncut.) 'What is more, I have a big machine nearly finished in there'—he indicated the laboratory—'and when that is put together I mean to have a journey on my own account.'

1. What is the main topic of the passage?

     _____

     _____

2. *What* does the author say about that topic?

     _____

     _____

3. *Why* does the author write about that topic?

     _____

     _____

The main topic of this passage is that a man has invented his own device for time travel. *What* does the author say about this topic? He has the narrator describe an experiment that the man conducts in which he claims to make a machine travel in time. Then the time traveler states that he intends to make a journey of his own. So *why* does the author write about this topic? Because the passage as a whole leads up to the Time Traveler's astonishing statement that he intends to make his own journey through time, it seems likely that the passage was written to introduce the fact that the Time Traveler will soon make this journey.

Now try this next passage, taken from *The Phantom of the Opera*, by Gaston Leroux.

The Opera ghost really existed. He was not, as was long believed, a creature of the imagination of the artists, the superstition of the managers, or a product of the absurd and impressionable brains of the young ladies of the ballet, their mothers, the box-keepers, the cloak-room attendants or the concierge. Yes, he existed in flesh and blood, although he assumed the complete appearance of a real phantom; that is to say, of a spectral shade.

When I began to ransack the archives of the National Academy of Music I was at once struck by the surprising coincidences between the phenomena ascribed to the "ghost" and the most extraordinary and fantastic tragedy that ever excited the Paris upper classes; and I soon conceived the idea that this tragedy might reasonably be explained by the phenomena in question. The events do not date more than thirty years back; and it would not be difficult to find at the present day, in the foyer of the ballet, old men of the highest respectability, men upon whose word one could absolutely rely, who would remember as though they happened yesterday the mysterious and dramatic conditions that attended the kidnapping of Christine Daae, the disappearance of the Vicomte de Chagny and the death of his elder brother, Count Philippe, whose body was found on the bank of the lake that exists in the lower cellars of the Opera on the Rue-Scribe side. But none of those witnesses had until that day thought that there was any reason for connecting the more or less legendary figure of the Opera ghost with that terrible story.

The truth was slow to enter my mind, puzzled by an inquiry that at every moment was complicated by events which, at first sight, might be looked upon as superhuman; and more than once I was within an ace of abandoning a task in which I was exhausting myself in the hopeless pursuit of a vain image. At last, I received the proof that my presentiments had not deceived me, and I was rewarded for all my efforts on the day when I acquired the certainty that the Opera ghost was more than a mere shade.

On that day, I had spent long hours over *The Memoirs of the Manager,* the light and frivolous work of the too-skeptical Moncharmin, who, during his term at the Opera, understood nothing of the mysterious behavior of the ghost and who was making all the fun of it that he could at the very moment when he became the first victim of the curious financial operation that went on inside the "magic envelope."

I had just left the library in despair, when I met the delightful acting-manager of our National Academy, who stood chatting on a landing with a lively and well-groomed little old man, to whom he introduced me gaily. The acting-manager knew all about my investigations and how eagerly and unsuccessfully I had been trying to discover the whereabouts of the examining magistrate in the famous Chagny case, M. Faure. Nobody knew what had become of him, alive or dead; and here he was back from Canada, where he had spent fifteen years, and the first thing he had done, on his return to Paris, was to come to the secretarial offices at the Opera and ask for a free seat. The little old man was M. Faure himself.

We spent a good part of the evening together and he told me the whole Chagny case as he had understood it at the time. He was bound to conclude in favor of the madness of the viscount and the accidental death of the elder brother, for lack of evidence to the contrary; but he was nevertheless persuaded that a terrible tragedy had taken place between the two brothers in connection with Christine Daaé. He could not tell me what became of Christine or the viscount. When I mentioned the ghost, he only laughed. He, too, had been told of the curious manifestations that seemed to point to the existence of an abnormal being, residing in one of the most mysterious corners of the Opera, and he knew the story of the envelope; but he had never seen anything in it worthy of his attention as magistrate in charge of the Chagny case, and it was as much as he had done to listen to the evidence of a witness who appeared of his own accord and declared that he had often met the ghost. This witness was none other than the man whom all Paris called the "Persian" and who was well-known to every subscriber to the Opera. The magistrate took him for a visionary.

I was immensely interested by this story of the Persian. I wanted, if there were still time, to find this valuable and eccentric witness. My luck began to improve and I discovered him in his little flat in the Rue de Rivoli, where he had lived ever since and where he died five months after my visit. I was at first inclined to be suspicious; but when the Persian had told me, with child-like candor, all that he knew about the ghost and had handed me the proofs of the ghost's existence—including the strange correspondence of Christine Daaé—to do as I pleased with, I was no longer able to doubt. No, the ghost was not a myth!

I have, I know, been told that this correspondence may have been forged from first to last by a man whose imagination had certainly been fed on the most seductive tales; but fortunately I discovered some of Christine's writing outside the famous bundle of letters and, on a comparison between the two, all my doubts were removed. I also went into the past history of the Persian and found that he was an upright man, incapable of inventing a story that might have defeated the ends of justice.

1.   What is the main topic of this passage?

    _____

    _____

2.   *What* does the author say about this topic?

    _____

    _____

3.   *Why* did the author write about this topic?

    _____

    _____

The main topic of the passage is the Opera ghost and the investigation conducted to find it. The narrator begins by explaining that the ghost really existed, and then goes on to explain the steps that he took in order to determine that the ghost was real, and the evidence that he found. He then once again states that he feels confident that the ghost existed. *Why* did the author write this passage, then? He must have written it in order to explain why the narrator could feel confident that the ghost was real and to provide evidence that the narrator was correct.

The passage below is an excerpt from *A Connecticut Yankee in King Arthur's Court.* Examine the passage and use the questions that follow to identify its primary purpose.

It was in Warwick Castle that I came across the curious stranger whom I am going to talk about. He attracted me by three things: his candid simplicity, his marvelous familiarity with ancient armor, and the restfulness of his company—for he did all the talking. We fell together, as modest people will, in the tail of the herd that was being shown through, and he at once began to say things which interested me. As he talked along, softly, pleasantly, flowingly, he seemed to drift away imperceptibly out of this world and time, and into some remote era and old forgotten country; and so he gradually wove such a spell about me that I seemed to move among the specters and shadows and dust and mold of a gray antiquity, holding speech with a relic of it! Exactly as I would speak of my nearest personal friends or enemies, or my most familiar neighbors, he spoke of Sir Bedivere, Sir Bors de Ganis, Sir Launcelot of the Lake, Sir Galahad, and all the other great names of the Table Round—and how old, old, unspeakably old and faded and dry and musty and ancient he came to look as he went on! Presently he turned to me and said, just as one might speak of the weather, or any other common matter—

"You know about transmigration of souls; do you know about transposition of epochs—and bodies?"

I said I had not heard of it. He was so little interested—just as when people speak of the weather—that he did not notice whether I made him any answer or not. There was half a moment of silence, immediately interrupted by the droning voice of the salaried tour guide:

"Ancient shirt of chain mail, date of the sixth century, time of King Arthur and the Round Table; said to have belonged to the knight Sir Sagramor le Desirous; observe the round hole through the chain-mail in the left breast; can't be accounted for; supposed to have been done with a bullet since invention of firearms—perhaps maliciously by Cromwell's soldiers."

My acquaintance smiled—not a modern smile, but one that must have gone out of general use many, many centuries ago—and muttered apparently to himself:

"As a matter of fact, I saw it done." Then, after a pause, added: "I did it myself."

By the time I had recovered from the electric surprise of this remark, he was gone.

1. What is the main topic of the passage?

    _____

    _____

2. *What* does the author say about that topic?

    _____

    _____

3.	*Why* does the author write about that topic?

_____

_____

Were you able to identify the primary purpose of the passage? Note that the main topic of the passage is the *curious stranger*. *What* does the author say about this topic? He has the narrator say that the stranger spoke of ancient people as if they were his *nearest personal friends or enemies*. He also says that the man appeared to become *old, unspeakably old and faded and dry and musty and ancient* as he spoke. Finally, he states that the man claimed to have shot a bullet through a set of ancient armor. Note that all of the facts about this man seem to suggest that he may have lived in the long distant past as well as in the present. *Why* does the author write about this topic? The purpose of the paragraph was to describe the narrator's encounter with a strange man who had somehow also lived hundreds of years earlier.

Shorter Is Better

Notice that you can often describe the purpose of an entire passage in just a few words. When you try to describe the purpose of a passage, rather than providing all of the details from the entire excerpt, try to focus on the big picture. Look for main ideas, main topics, and the overarching reasons why authors write, rather than for specifics and minutiae. This approach will help you when you tackle reading questions on standardized tests such as the SAT and ACT, because the answers to primary purpose questions on these tests tend to be only a few words long. If you can create a good, short paraphrase of a passage, you'll be much more likely to be able to recognize a good, short paraphrase in one of the answer choices.

Finding the Primary Purpose of SAT and ACT Reading Passages

Now that you've had some practice finding the purposes of passages, put your skills to use on this non-fiction excerpt below. As you read, look for the big picture. See whether you can identify the main topic, and focus on what the author says about that topic. Finally, in your own words, try to explain *why* the author wrote the passage. Once you have a firm grasp of the primary purpose of the passage, go to the answer choices and try to identify the choice that describes the passage's main purpose.

After years of such strenuous critical work, the mind becomes molded in a certain cast. It is as impossible for me to put aside the habit of the literary critic as it would be for a hunter who had spent his whole life in the woods to be content in a great city. So when I started out on this trip around the world, the critical apparatus which I had used in getting at the heart of books was applied to the people and the places along this great girdle about the globe.

Much of the benefit of foreign travel depends upon the reading that one has done. For years my eager curiosity about places had led me to read everything printed about the Orient and the South Seas. Add to this the stories which were brought into a newspaper office by globe trotters and adventurers, and you have an equipment which made me at times seem to be merely revising impressions made on an earlier journey. When you talk with a man who has spent ten or twenty years in Japan or China or the Straits Settlements, you cannot fail to get something of the color of life in those strange lands, especially if you have the newspaper training which impels you to ask questions and to drag out of your informant everything of human interest that the reader will care to know.

This newspaper instinct, which is developed by training but which one must possess in large measure before he can be successful in journalism, seizes upon everything and transmutes it into "copy" for the printer. To have taken this journey without setting down every day my impressions of places and people would have been a tiresome experience. What seemed labor to others who had not had my special training was as the breath in my nostrils. Even in the debilitating heat of the tropics it was always a pastime, never a task, to put into words my ideas of the historic places which I knew so well from years of reading and which I had just seen. And the richer the background of history, the greater was my enjoyment in painting with words full of color a picture of my impressions, for the benefit of those who were not able to share my pleasure in the actual sight of these famous places of the Far East.

10. The primary purpose of the passage is to

   a) describe the benefits of traveling to the Orient and the South Seas
   b) demonstrate the advantages of pursuing a career in newspaper editing
   c) explain how one person's background influenced that person's outlook and actions while traveling
   d) define the term "newspaper instinct" and illustrate strenuous nature of a writer's life
   e) contrast the lives of adventurers and globetrotters with those of the readers

The topic of this passage is the way in which the habits of a writer related to his travel experiences. So, *what* does the author say about this topic? In the first paragraph, he states that *It is as impossible for me to put aside the habit of the literary critic as it would be for a hunter who had spent his whole life in the woods to be content in a great city.* He then explains that he applied the critical thinking that he normally used to evaluate books to the people and places that he encountered during his travels. In the second paragraph, he says that in the past he had talked with individuals who had traveled all over the world, and then he explains that *newspaper training ... impels you to ask questions and to drag out of your informant everything of human interest that the reader will care to know.* In the third paragraph, he discusses the *newspaper instinct,* and says that this instinct impels him to record *impressions of places and people.* Therefore, the passage as a whole is discussing the ways in which his background in journalism affected his actions and thoughts as he traveled. So, *why* did the author write about this topic? He must have written this passage to explain how his background in journalism affected what he did and what he thought as he traveled. Now examine the answer choices. The passage does mention *the benefits of foreign travel,* but it does not discuss the benefits of specifically traveling to the Orient and the South Seas, although it does mention these places by name. Therefore, choice (a) does not describe the primary purpose of the passage, and is not the credited answer. The passage does discuss the author's background in journalism, and it also mentions some of the positive ways in which the man's experiences in journalism affected his life. However, the passage does not specifically mention careers in editing (although it does talk about his career in writing). Additionally, the passage does not focus on the general advantages of pursuing a literary career; it only focuses on how the author's literary background affected his views and actions as he traveled. Thus, choice (b) is incorrect. Choice (c) agrees with the answer mentioned earlier; the author wrote the passage to explain how his background in journalism affected what he did and what he thought as he traveled. Therefore, choice (c) is the correct answer. Now consider choice (d). The passage does include the term *newspaper instinct,* but the focus of the passage is not on defining that term. Additionally, while the introductory paragraph does mention *years of strenuous critical work,* the passage as a whole does not focus on the ways in which writing is a difficult career. Therefore, you can eliminate choice (d). Finally, while the passage does mention *adventurers* and *globetrotters,* it does not compare the lives of those individuals to your life and the lives of other readers, so you can eliminate choice (e).

Now that you have developed your critical reading skills in finding the primary purposes of sentences, paragraphs, and passages, try the drill questions that follow. As you tackle each drill, remember: If you're looking for the primary purpose of a work, always ask *what* the author says and *why* he or she says it!

Practice 1

Read the sentences below, and use the accompanying questions to find the primary purpose of each one. Write down your answers. Answers and explanations to all practice activities are located at the end of the Practice section. Check your answers for accuracy.

1. In Argentina, for example, inflation is expected to reach 25% annually by December of 2014.

   What does the author say?

   _____

   _____

   Why does he or she make that statement?

   _____

   _____

2. We have no exact knowledge of the number of auxiliary Roman troops during Augustus' time, but they probably came to be as numerous as the legionaries.

   What does the author say?

   _____

   _____

   Why does he or she make that statement?

   _____

   _____

3. The fact, however, that Jane Austen had not earned more than £700 from her novels by the time of her death shows that she never became a really popular author in her lifetime.

   What does the author say?

   _____

   _____

   Why does he or she make that statement?

   _____

   _____

4. It has often been said that in Chinese painting, perspective is ignored. Nothing is further from the truth. This error arises from the fact that we have confused one system of perspective with perspective as a whole. There are as many systems of perspective as there are conventional laws for them.

What does the author say in the first sentence of the paragraph?

_____

_____

What does the author discuss immediately after this sentence?

_____

_____

Consider how these thoughts fit together. *Why* did he or she write the first sentence of the paragraph?

_____

_____

The Yellow Room! Who now remembers this affair which caused so much ink to flow fifteen years ago? Events are so quickly forgotten in Paris. Has not the very name of the Nayves
Line trial and the tragic history of the death of little Menaldo
5 passed out of mind? And yet the public attention was so deeply interested in the details of the trial that the occurrence of a ministerial crisis was completely unnoticed at the time. Now The Yellow Room trial, which preceded that of the Nayves by some years, made far more noise. The entire world hung for
10 months over this obscure problem—the most obscure, it seems to me, that has ever challenged the perspicacity of our police or taxed the conscience of our judges. The solution of the problem baffled everybody who tried to find it. That is, in truth—I am permitted to say, because there cannot be any author's vanity
15 in all this, since I do nothing more than transcribe facts on which an exceptional documentation enables me to throw a new light—that is because, in truth, I do not know that, in the domain of reality or imagination, one can discover or recall to mind anything comparable, in its mystery, with the natural
20 mystery of The Yellow Room.

5. The primary purpose of lines 3–5 (*Has not the very name … of mind?*) is to

a) illustrate a contrast between two trials.
b) provide an example that supports a previous statement.
c) demonstrate the fickle nature of mystery writers.
d) question the need for deeper inquiry into a tragic history.
e) criticize the way in which a certain investigation was handled.

Practice 2

Read the paragraphs below, and use the accompanying questions to find the primary purpose of each one. Write down your answers.

Passage 1

Few literatures have exerted so profound an influence upon the literary history of other peoples as the poetry of the Provençal troubadours. Attaining the highest point of technical perfection in the last half of the twelfth and the early years of the thirteenth century, Provençal poetry was already popular in Italy and Spain when the Albigeois crusade devastated the south of France and scattered the troubadours abroad or forced them to seek other means of livelihood. The earliest lyric poetry of Italy is Provençal in all but language; almost as much may be said of Portugal and Galicia; Catalonian troubadours continued to write in Provençal until the fourteenth century. The lyric poetry of the "trouvères" in Northern France was deeply influenced both in form and spirit by troubadour poetry, and traces of this influence are perceptible even in early middle-English lyrics. Finally, the German minnesingers knew and appreciated troubadour lyrics, and imitations or even translations of Provençal poems may be found in Heinrich von Morungen, Friedrich von Hausen, and many others. Hence, the poetry of the Provençal troubadours is a subject of first-rate importance to the student of comparative literature.

What is the main topic of the paragraph?

_____

_____

What does the author say about that topic?

_____

_____

Why does the author write about that topic?

_____

_____

Passage 2

The Gallic genius is eminently a social one, but it is, of all others, the most difficult to reproduce. The subtle grace of manner, the magic of spoken words, are gone with the moment. The conversations of two centuries ago are today like champagne which has lost its sparkle. We may recall their tangible forms—the facts, the accessories, the thoughts, even the words, but the flavor is not there. It is the volatile essence of gaiety and wit that especially characterizes French society. It glitters from a thousand facets, it surprises us in a thousand delicate turns of thought, it appears in countless movements and shades of expression. But it refuses to be imprisoned. Hence the impossibility of catching the essential spirit of the salons. We know something of the men and women who frequented them, as they have left many records of themselves. We have numerous pictures of their social life from which we may partially reconstruct it and trace its influence. But the nameless attraction that held for so long a period the most serious men of letters as well as the merry world still eludes us.

What is the main topic of the paragraph?

_____

_____

What does the author say about that topic?

_____

_____

Why does the author write about that topic?

_____

_____

Passage 3

My uncle was a very learned man. Now most persons in this category supply themselves with information, as peddlers do with goods, for the benefit of others, and lay up stores in order to diffuse them abroad for the benefit of society in general. Not so my excellent uncle, Professor Hardwigg; he studied, he consumed the midnight oil, he pored over heavy tomes, and digested huge quartos and folios in order to keep the knowledge acquired to himself.

What is the main topic of the paragraph?

_____

_____

What does the author say about that topic?

_____

_____

Why does the author write about that topic?

_____

_____

Passage 4

Wagner's music, more than any other, is the sign and symbol of the nineteenth century. The men to whom it was disclosed, and who first sought to refuse, and then accepted it, passionately, without reservations, found in it their truth. It came to their ears as the sound of their own voices. It was the common, the universal tongue. Not alone on Germany, not alone on Europe, but on every quarter of the globe that had developed coal-power civilization, the music of Wagner descended with the formative might of the perfect image. Men of every race and continent knew it to be of themselves as much as was their hereditary and racial music, and went out to it as to their own adventure. And wherever music reappeared, whether under the hand of the Japanese or the semi-African or the Yankee, it seemed to be growing from Wagner as the bright shoots of the fir sprout from the dark ones grown the previous year. A whole world, for a period, came to use his idiom. His dream was recognized during his very lifetime as an integral portion of the consciousness of the entire race.

What is the main topic of the paragraph?

_____

_____

What does the author say about that topic?

_____

_____

Why does the author write about that topic?

_____

_____

Passage 5

"Are we rising again?" "No. On the contrary." "Are we descending?" "Worse than that, captain! we are falling!" "For Heaven's sake heave out the ballast!" "There! the last sack is empty!" "Does the balloon rise?" "No!" "I hear a noise like the dashing of waves. The sea is below the car! It cannot be more than 500 feet from us!" "Overboard with every weight! ... everything!"

Such were the loud and startling words which resounded through the air, above the vast watery desert of the Pacific, about four o'clock in the evening of the 23rd of March, 1865.

Few can possibly have forgotten the terrible storm from the northeast, in the middle of the equinox of that year. The tempest raged without intermission from the 18th to the 26th of March. Its ravages were terrible in America, Europe, and Asia, covering a distance of eighteen hundred miles, and extending obliquely to the equator from the thirty-fifth north parallel to the fortieth south parallel. Towns were overthrown, forests uprooted, coasts devastated by the mountains of water which were precipitated on them, vessels cast on the shore, which the published accounts numbered by hundreds, whole districts leveled by waterspouts which destroyed everything they passed over, several thousand people crushed on land or drowned at sea; such were the traces of its fury, left by this devastating tempest. It surpassed in disasters those which so frightfully ravaged Havana and Guadeloupe, one on the 25th of October, 1810, the other on the 26th of July, 1825.

But while so many catastrophes were taking place on land and at sea, a drama not less exciting was being enacted in the agitated air.

In fact, a balloon, as a ball might be carried on the summit of a waterspout, had been taken into the circling movement of a column of air and had traversed space at the rate of ninety miles an hour, turning round and round as if seized by some aerial maelstrom.

Beneath the lower point of the balloon swung a car, containing five passengers, scarcely visible in the midst of the thick vapor mingled with spray which hung over the surface of the ocean.

Whence, it may be asked, had come that plaything of the tempest? From what part of the world did it rise? It surely could not have started during the storm. But the storm had raged five days already, and the first symptoms were manifested on the 18th. It cannot be doubted that the balloon came from a great distance, for it could not have traveled less than two thousand miles in twenty-four hours.

5. The primary purpose of the third paragraph is to

    a) describe the damage that the storm caused in Havana and Guadeloupe
    b) discuss a series of incidents that occurred in a hot air balloon
    c) set up a comparison between events occurring on land and at sea and in the air
    d) trace the cause of a storm that killed several thousand people and uprooted forests

Practice 3

Read the passages below, and answer the questions that follow each passage.

Passage 1

The fortune left by his grandfather, who had been one of those chieftains on the smaller scale of his day, had descended to him with accretion through his father, who during a long life had quietly continued to lend money and never had margined a stock. Manderson, who had at no time known what it was to be without large sums to his hand, should have been altogether of that newer American plutocracy which is steadied by the tradition and habit of great wealth. But it was not so. While his nurture and education had taught him European ideas of a rich man's proper external circumstance; while they had rooted in him an instinct for quiet magnificence, the larger costliness which does not shriek of itself with a thousand tongues; there had been handed on to him nevertheless much of the Forty-Niner and financial buccaneer, his forbear. During that first period of his business career which had been called his early bad manner, he had been little more than a gambler of genius, his hand against every man's—an infant prodigy—who brought to the enthralling pursuit of speculation a brain better endowed than any opposed to it. At St Helena it was laid down that war is *une belle occupation*; and so the young Manderson had found the multitudinous and complicated dog-fight of the Stock Exchange of New York.

Then came his change. At his father's death, when Manderson was thirty years old, some new revelation of the power and the glory of the god he served seemed to have come upon him. With the sudden, elastic adaptability of his nation he turned to steady labour in his father's banking business, closing his ears to the sound of the battles of the Street. In a few years he came to control all the activity of the great firm whose unimpeached conservatism, safety, and financial weight lifted it like a cliff above the angry sea of the markets. All mistrust founded on the performances of his youth had vanished. He was quite plainly a different man. How the change came about none could with authority say, but there was a story of certain last words spoken by his father, whom alone he had respected and perhaps loved.

He began to tower above the financial situation. Soon his name was current in the bourses of the world. One who spoke the name of Manderson called up a vision of all that was broad-based and firm in the vast wealth of the United States. He planned great combinations of capital, drew together and centralized industries of continental scope, financed with unerring judgment the large designs of state or of private enterprise. Many a time when he 'took hold' to smash a strike, or to federate the ownership of some great field of labour, he sent ruin upon a multitude of tiny homes; and if miners or steelworkers or cattlemen defied him and invoked disorder, he could be more lawless and ruthless than they. But this was done in the pursuit of legitimate business ends. Tens of thousands of the poor might curse his name, but the financier and the speculator execrated him no more. He stretched a hand to protect or to manipulate the power of wealth in every corner of the country. Forcible, cold, and unerring, in all he did he ministered to the national lust for magnitude; and a grateful country surnamed him the Colossus.

What is the main topic of the passage?

_____

_____

What does the author say about that topic?

_____

_____

Why does the author write about that topic?

_____

_____

Passage 2

I had now arrived at that particular point of my walk where four roads met—the road to Hampstead, along which I had returned, the road to Finchley, the road to West End, and the road back to London. I had mechanically turned in this latter direction, and was strolling along the lonely high-road—idly wondering, I remember, what the Cumberland young ladies would look like—when, in one moment, every drop of blood in my body was brought to a stop by the touch of a hand laid lightly and suddenly on my shoulder from behind me.

I turned on the instant, with my fingers tightening round the handle of my stick.

There, in the middle of the broad bright high-road—there, as if it had that moment sprung out of the earth or dropped from the heaven—stood the figure of a solitary Woman, dressed from head to foot in white garments, her face bent in grave inquiry on mine, her hand pointing to the dark cloud over London, as I faced her.

I was far too seriously startled by the suddenness with which this extraordinary apparition stood before me, in the dead of night and in that lonely place, to ask what she wanted. The strange woman spoke first.

"Is that the road to London?" she said.

I looked attentively at her, as she put that singular question to me. It was then nearly one o'clock. All I could discern distinctly by the moonlight was a colorless, youthful face, meager and sharp to look at about the cheeks and chin; large, grave, wistfully attentive eyes; nervous, uncertain lips; and light hair of a pale, brownish-yellow hue. There was nothing wild, nothing immodest in her manner: it was quiet and self-controlled, a little melancholy and a little touched by suspicion; not exactly the manner of a lady, and, at the same time, not the manner of a woman in the humblest rank of life. The voice, little as I had yet heard of it, had something curiously still and mechanical in its tones, and the utterance was remarkably rapid. She held a small bag in her hand: and her dress—bonnet, shawl, and gown all of white—was, so far as I could guess, certainly not composed of very delicate or very expensive materials. Her figure was slight, and rather above the average height—her gait and actions free from the slightest approach to extravagance. This was all that I could observe of her in the dim light and under the perplexingly strange circumstances of our meeting. What sort of a woman she was, and how she came to be out alone in the high-road, an hour after midnight, I altogether failed to guess. The one thing of which I felt certain was, that the grossest of mankind could not have misconstrued her motive in speaking, even at that suspiciously late hour and in that suspiciously lonely place.

"Did you hear me?" she said, still quietly and rapidly, and without the least fretfulness or impatience. "I asked if that was the way to London."

"Yes," I replied, "that is the way: it leads to St. John's Wood and the Regent's Park. You must excuse my not answering you before. I was rather startled by your sudden appearance in the road; and I am, even now, quite unable to account for it."

"You don't suspect me of doing anything wrong, do you? I have done nothing wrong. I have met with an accident— I am very unfortunate in being here alone so late. Why do you suspect me of doing wrong?"

She spoke with unnecessary earnestness and agitation, and shrank back from me several paces. I did my best to reassure her.

"Pray don't suppose that I have any idea of suspecting you," I said, "or any other wish than to be of assistance to you, if I can. I only wondered at your appearance in the road, because it seemed to me to be empty the instant before I saw you."

She turned, and pointed back to a place at the junction of the road to London and the road to Hampstead, where there was a gap in the hedge.

"I heard you coming," she said, "and hid there to see what sort of man you were, before I risked speaking. I doubted and feared about it till you passed; and then I was obliged to steal after you, and touch you."

Steal after me and touch me? Why not call to me? Strange, to say the least of it.

2. The primary purpose of the passage is to

    a)   criticize the actions of a young woman
    b)   explain how an apparition appeared
    c)   depict a suspicious character
    d)   detail a course of action
    e)   describe an unusual encounter

ANSWERS AND EXPLANATIONS

Practice 1

1. *What* the author says that inflation in Argentina is expected to reach 25%. *Why* does the author make that statement? Notice that the sentence includes the words *for example*. Therefore, the author must mention Argentina's inflation in order to provide an example of a country in which annual inflation will likely increase.

2. *What* the author says is that the exact number of auxiliary Roman troops during a certain time is unknown, but that the troops were probably numerous. *Why* did the author write this sentence? He must have written this sentence to emphasize an uncertainty, and to provide an estimate.

3. *What* the author states is that Jane Austen had not earned very much from her novels by the time that she died. *Why* does he make that statement? He says that the fact that she had not earned much *shows that she never became a really popular author during her lifetime*. Therefore, the author must have written this sentence in order to present evidence that Jane Austen was not a truly popular author during her own lifetime.

4. *What* the author says in the first paragraph is that many people have claimed *that in Chinese painting, perspective is ignored*. Immediately after the author makes this statement, he then goes on to explain that this claim is wrong. He then explains the origins of that claim. So, *why* did the author write the first sentence? He must have written it in order to present a point of view that he would later argue against.

5. **Choice (b).** In the sentence in question, the author states that the name of the Nayves trial and the death of Menaldo have been forgotten. Notice that immediately before that sentence, he states that *Events are so quickly forgotten in Paris*. Immediately after that sentence, he states that at the time of the Nayves trial, the public was extremely interested in the details of the trial. So, *why* did the author write the sentence in question? Because the sentence contains an example of a trial that the public was deeply interested in when it occurred, but quickly forgot afterward, the author must have written the sentence in order to provide an example that supported his statement that events were soon forgotten in Paris. Now examine your answer choices. The paragraph does mention two trials—the Nayves trial and the Yellow Room trial—but because the paragraph discusses the fact that they were both quickly forgotten, the paragraph emphasizes the similarities, rather than the contrasts, between the two trials. Therefore, choice (a) is not the credited answer. The statement

immediately before the sentence in question is that *Events are so quickly forgotten in Paris.* Because the sentence in question provides support for that statement by giving an example of an event that was famous when it occurred, but was soon forgotten, the sentence does provide an example that supports a previous statement. Therefore, choice (b) is the credited answer. The sentence demonstrates the fickle nature of public interest, but does not mention the fickle nature of mystery writers, so choice (c) is not the correct answer. Because the sentence mentions a tragic history, but does not question the need for deeper inquiry into that history, you can eliminate choice (d). Finally, the sentence does mention a trial and a death, but does not offer any criticism regarding the way in which the investigation of the death or the tragedy was handled, so choice (e) is incorrect.

Practice 2

Passage 1: The main topic of the paragraph is the poetry of the Provençal troubadours. *What* the author says about the troubadours is that they have had a profound effect on literary history. He then goes on to provide examples of the ways in which they have affected history. *Why* does the author write about this topic? Notice that the final sentence of the paragraph reads, *Hence, the poetry of the Provençal troubadours is a subject of first-rate importance to the student of comparative literature.* Therefore, the author must have written the paragraph to explain why the students of comparative literature should study the poetry of Provençal troubadours.

Passage 2: The main topic of the paragraph is the essence of French society and salons. *What* the author says about the French society and salons is that their atmosphere is *difficult to reproduce.* She explains that French conversations may be reproduced, but *the flavor is not there.* She goes on to state that we know about the men and women who went to the salons and that we have pictures of their social life, but a full understanding of their society *still eludes us. Why* did the author write about that topic? Because the author focuses on *the impossibility of catching the essential spirit of the salons,* her purpose in writing must have been to state that catching the essential spirit of the salons is impossible and to explain why catching that spirit is impossible.

Passage 3: The main topic of this paragraph is Professor Hardwigg. *What* the author says about this topic is that Professor Hardwigg was a very learned man who spent much time studying. *Why* does the author write about this topic? Notice that he contrasts Professor Hardwigg with other learned men. He says that such men studied in order to benefit others, but *not so my learned uncle.* He explains that instead Professor Hardwigg studied *in order to keep the knowledge acquired to himself.* Therefore, the purpose of the passage must be to provide a contrast between the professor and other learned men.

Passage 4: The main topic of this paragraph is Wagner's music. *What* the author states about that topic is that Wagner's music was *the sign and symbol of the nineteenth century.* He then goes on to state that Wagner's music spread to *every quarter of the globe that had developed coal-power civilization*, and Wagner's dream became *an integral portion of the consciousness of the entire race. Why* did the author write about this topic? He must have written it to demonstrate the powerful effect that Wagner's music had on the world.

Passage 5: **Choice** (c). The main topic of the third paragraph is the terrible storm that occurred in the Northeast. *What* the author says about that storm is that it *raged without intermission* and that *its ravages were terrible.* In the paragraph immediately preceding, the author discusses events occurring in the air. In the paragraph immediately following, the author says that *a drama not less exciting was being enacted in the agitated air.* Because both the paragraph immediately before the third paragraph and the paragraph immediately after the third paragraph discuss events occurring in the air, the author must have written the third paragraph in order to relate it in some way to the events occurring in the air. Notice that the fourth paragraph begins by contrasting events occurring in land and at sea with the events occurring in the air. Therefore, the author must have introduced the events occurring on land and at sea—the events discussed in the third paragraph—in order to set up that contrast. The paragraph mentions that storms caused damage in Havana and Guadeloupe, but because the purpose of the paragraph is not to describe that damage, choice (a) is not the credited answer. Note too that the passage states that Havana was ravaged by a storm in 1810, while Guadeloupe was ravaged in 1825. Therefore, the two areas were not ravaged by the same storm. The events that occurred in the hot air balloon are described in the paragraphs before and after the third paragraph but are not discussed in the third paragraph, so choice (b) is incorrect. Choice (c) correctly identifies the purpose of the paragraph as described above and is the credited answer. The third paragraph mentions that the storm killed several thousand people but does not trace the cause of the storm, so choice (c) is incorrect.

Practice 3

Passage 1: The main topic of the passage is a man named Manderson. *What* the author says about him is that when he was younger, he was a *financial buccaneer and a a gambler of genius,* but that when his father died, Manderson *turned to steady labour and came to control all of the activity* in a large firm. The author goes on to state that Manderson *began to tower above the financial situation* and was eventually called *the Colossus. Why* does the author write about this topic? Because the passage as a whole focuses on how Manderson developed into an important financial figure, the purpose of the passage must have been to describe how Manderson developed into such a figure.

Passage 2: **Choice (e).** The main topic of the passage is a meeting between a man and a young woman. *What* the author says about the topic is that the young woman startled the man when she appeared suddenly; she was dressed completely in white. He also describes his meeting with the young woman as *strange, to say the least of it*. *Why* does the author write about this topic? Because the passage focuses on the strange meeting between the man and the woman, the purpose of the passage must be to describe an unusual meeting. The narrator does not criticize the young woman, so choice (a) is incorrect. The young woman does explain that the reason that she seemed to appear suddenly is because she had been hiding behind a hedge, and she waited until she had evaluated the man's appearance before she stepped out. However, because this explanation is not the main focus of the passage, choice (b) is not the credited answer. The passage does say that the young woman was *a little touched by suspicion;* however, this suggests that the woman viewed others with suspicion, not that *she* was a suspicious character. Therefore, you can eliminate choice (c). Because the passage does not detail any course of action, choice (d) is incorrect. Choice (e) correctly identifies the purpose of the passage as discussed above and is the correct answer.

SUMMARY

In order to find the purposes of sentences, ask yourself the following questions:

1. *What* does the author say?
2. What does the author discuss immediately before this sentence?
3. What does the author discuss immediately after this sentence?
4. Consider how these thoughts fit together. *Why* does he or she make that statement?

In order to find the purposes of paragraphs, ask yourself the following questions:

1. What is the main topic of the paragraph?
2. *What* does the author say about that topic?
3. What does the author discuss in the paragraph immediately before the paragraph?
4. What does the author discuss in the paragraph immediately following the paragraph?
5. Consider how these thoughts relate to one another. *Why* did the author write the paragraph?

In order to find the purposes of passages, look at the big picture. Ask yourself the following questions:

1. What is the main topic of this passage?
2. *What* does the author say about this topic?
3. *Why* did the author write about this topic?

Remember: The key to finding the purpose of a piece of writing is to find out not just what the author wrote, but *why* he or she wrote it!

Conquering Hard Passages

Author: Alice Swan

MAKING SENSE OF HARD PASSAGES

Let's look at a sentence.

The mercurial, tawny fox bounds over the indolent canine.

You are probably wondering what this sentence means. There is a lot of hard vocabulary in it, and if you're like most people, you stop at the word *mercurial* and think to yourself, "I've never heard that word before—what in the world does it mean?" It doesn't help, of course, that the definition of the next word, *tawny*, doesn't instantly come to mind either. When there are two words in a row whose meanings you don't understand, making sense of the sentence can be quite difficult. If you were to see this sentence in a reading passage on a standardized test, you would likely gloss over the two words in a row that don't make sense to you.

But do you have to? Absolutely not! In order to help you make sense of this sentence, let's talk about the way most sentences are written. The main parts of a sentence are the **subject**, or noun (person, place, or thing that a sentence is about), and the *predicate*. We often think of the predicate as being the verb, but it's a little bit more than that. The predicate is the part of the sentence that *tells us about the subject*. It always contains a **verb**, or action, and it usually also contains an **object** (the thing that receives the action of the verb).

These are the three main parts of most sentences.

1. *Subject*: the person, place, or thing that a sentence is about
2. *Verb*: the action
3. *Object*: the thing that receives the action of the verb

Here's another example.

Alexander went to school.

1. What is the subject? *Alexander*
2. What is the verb? *went*
3. What is the object? *to school*

Let's examine another version of this sentence.

> *Even though he had not finished his History project, Alexander reluctantly went to school on Monday, where he received a lecture from his teacher on the importance of deadlines.*

murza08/Shutterstock.com

There is a lot more information in the second version of the sentence. However, notice how the main parts are still the same: The subject is still *Alexander*, the verb is still *went*, and the object is still *to school*.

Shutterstock.com

This second example of Alexander going to school doesn't have a lot of tough vocabulary like our first sentence had, but it illustrates an idea that can help us make sense of a sentence like the first one: If you run into a tough sentence, look for the three main parts. Have you ever seen someone preparing to cook a piece of meat by cutting off the fat to get to the good part? You can do the same thing with a long sentence. You can trim the fat—or the extra descriptive words—away from the main parts to get at the main meaning.

Let's look at that first example again.

> *The mercurial, tawny fox bounds over the indolent canine.*

If we trim the fat, we end up with

> *The … fox … bounds over the … canine.*

The words we cut out do add detail to the sentence, but the three main parts are the most important and convey the main meaning of the sentence. This is an excellent place to start when faced with a long, complicated sentence.

Practice: Trim the Fat

Find the subject, verb, and object in each of the following sentences. Write down a simpler version of each sentence: You may need to include a little more than those three main parts to get the basic meaning in each sentence. Check your answers at the end of the drill.

1. Wild pigs in Hawaii, which first arrived on the islands with Polynesian settlers over 1,200 years ago, are now a major threat to the delicate native ecosystem because of their destructive foraging habits.

   Subject: _____

   Verb: _____

   Object: _____

   Simple version: _____

2. While still an undergraduate at Yale, Maya Lin, the youngest daughter of Chinese immigrants, won the open competition for the design of the Vietnam Veterans Memorial in Washington, D.C., the first of many such honors she has subsequently received.

   Subject: _____

   Verb: _____

   Object: _____

   Simple version: _____

3. The curious children peeking over the sides of the boats out on the river in great numbers for the holiday weekend seemed to be mocking Sophie, as she sat on shore and glumly stared at her half-submerged rowboat.

   Subject: _____

   Verb: _____

   Object: _____

   Joakim Lloyd Raboff/
   Shutterstock.com

   Simple version: _____

4. Two different inventors, Frank Whittle in Britain and Hans von Ohain in Germany, simultaneously developed the jet engine, which has become standard apparatus in modern aircraft, in the 1930s.

   Subject: _____

   Verb: _____

   Object: _____

   Simple version: _____

5. Alfred Nobel, who invented dynamite as a safer alternative to earlier explosives that had burned down his factory two times, founded the Nobel Prizes to counteract the reputation he had earned as a "merchant of death" because of his success in the explosives business.

   Subject: _____

   Verb: _____

   Object: _____

   Simple version: _____

6. The major reason time-turners are closely regulated by the Ministry of Magic is that the magic related to time travel is unstable, and the potential for a catastrophic mistake, such as a the accidental death of one's past or future self, is high.

   Subject: _____

   Verb: _____

   Object: _____

   Simple version: _____

7. In 1572, a pug named Pompey saved the life of William the Silent, Prince of Orange, by barking at the approach of Spanish troops who had come to assassinate the prince while he slept.

   Subject: _____

   Verb: _____

   Object: _____

   Simple version: _____

8. Anakin's first prosthesis, which was a replacement for the right arm he lost in a fight with Dooku, was connected to his body by a synthennet neural interface, which allowed him to register feeling in the mechanical limb.

   Subject: _____

   Verb: _____

   Object: _____

   Simple version: _____

Answers and Explanations: Trim the Fat

The object of this drill is to cut out at much as you can without losing the important parts of the sentence. If your answers include more information than these answers do, that's fine. If you're not sure whether a phrase is important, it's best to keep it in the sentence.

1. Wild pigs in Hawaii, which first arrived on the islands with Polynesian settlers over 1,200 years ago, are now a major threat to the delicate native ecosystem because of their destructive foraging habits.

    Subject: wild pigs
    Verb: are
    Object: a threat

    Simple version: <u>Wild pigs in Hawaii are a threat to the ecosystem.</u>

    Trim the fat:

    - Phrases that start with the word *which* are not essential to the meaning of a sentence and can be ignored, so we can cut "which first arrived … years ago."
    - Extra adjectives (those are descriptive words such as *beautiful, blue,* and *flamin' hot*) can often be cut to get at the main idea of a sentence. Here we cut "major" from in front of "threat" and "delicate native" from in front of "ecosystem."
    - Sometimes a whole phrase is used to describe something. Just as extra adjectives can be cut, so can extra descriptive phrases. In this sentence, the phrase "because of their destructive foraging habits" adds detail to the sentence, but we get the big picture without it.

    But don't trim:

    - The information that tells us where the pigs are and what they threaten—these are important details in this sentence.

2. While still an undergraduate at Yale, Maya Lin, the youngest daughter of Chinese immigrants, won the open competition for the design of the Vietnam Veterans Memorial in Washington, D.C., the first of many such honors she has subsequently received.

    Subject: Maya Lin
    Verb: won
    Object: the competition

    Simple version: <u>Maya Lin won the competition for the design of the Vietnam Veterans Memorial.</u>

Trim the fat:

- Phrases set off from the rest of the sentence with commas can often be trimmed. They can appear in a variety of places in a sentence: the beginning ("While still an undergraduate at Yale,"), the middle ("..., the youngest daughter of Chinese immigrants,"), or the end ("..., the first of many such honors she has subsequently received.")

But don't trim:

- A really simple version of this sentence would be "Maya Lin won the competition." But because the word *the* appears in front of *competition*, we need to know which competition it is that she won, so keep the prepositional phrase "for the design ... Memorial."

3. The curious children peeking over the sides of the boats out on the river in great numbers for the holiday weekend seemed to be mocking Sophie, as she sat on shore and glumly stared at her half-submerged rowboat.

    Subject: the children
    Verb: seemed to be mocking
    Object: Sophie

    Simple version: <u>The children seemed to be mocking Sophie.</u>

    Trim the fat:

    - This sentence has lots of prepositional phrases. Prepositions are words that indicate relationships between things. The prepositions in this sentence are *over, of, out, on, in, for,* and *at*. Many prepositional phrases (such as *over the sides* and *out on the river*) can be cut from a sentence without losing essential information.
    - We can cut the extra adjective "curious."
    - There's a descriptive phrase set off by a comma at the end of this sentence ("as she sat ... rowboat.") that can be ignored.

4. Two different inventors, Frank Whittle in Britain and Hans von Ohain in Germany, simultaneously developed the jet engine, which has become standard apparatus in modern aircraft, in the 1930s.

    Subject: two inventors
    Verb: developed
    Object: the jet engine

    Simple version: <u>Two inventors developed the jet engine.</u>

Trim the fat:

- The names of the inventors, which are set off from the rest of the sentence by commas, are unnecessary.
- Extra adjective alert! We can ignore "simultaneously." It adds detail but is not crucial to understanding the basic idea of the sentence.
- There's that pesky "which" phrase again, describing the jet engine. Get rid of it.
- And wouldn't you know it, an unnecessary prepositional phrase ("in the 1930s") tops it all off. Get rid of that too.

5. Alfred Nobel, who invented dynamite as a safer alternative to earlier explosives that had burned down his factory two times, founded the Nobel Prizes to counteract the reputation he had earned as a "merchant of death" because of his success in the explosives business.

    Subject: Alfred Nobel
    Verb: founded
    Object: the Nobel Prizes

    Simple version: <u>Alfred Nobel founded the Nobel Prizes.</u>

    Trim the fat:

    - The phrase that starts "who invented …" is set off from the rest of the sentence by commas—get rid of it.
    - The whole end of the sentence, starting with "to counteract" is a long string of prepositional phrases that give us more detail but aren't essential to the basic idea of the sentence.

6. The major reason time-turners are closely regulated by the Ministry of Magic is that the magic related to time travel is highly unstable, and the potential for a catastrophic mistake, such as a the accidental death of one's past or future self, is high.

    Subject: the reason
    Verb: is
    Object: the magic is unstable

    Simple version: <u>The reason time-turners are regulated is that the magic is unstable.</u>

Trim the fat:

- The extra adjective "major" and the extra adverb "closely" can be ignored.
- So can the extra prepositional phrase ("by the Ministry of Magic") and the extra descriptive phrase ("related to time travel").
- The whole second half of this sentence is extra explanation. The word *and* tells us that the second half will agree with the first half; it's not going to make a whole new point. The words *such as* tell us that we're about to read an example. An example can further illustrate a point but isn't the main idea. This whole second part of the sentence is non-essential.

But don't trim:

- "The reason is that the magic is unstable" and "time turners are regulated." By itself, *the reason* is unclear; we also need to know what it refers to.

7. In 1572, a pug named Pompey saved the life of William the Silent, Prince of Orange, by barking at the approach of Spanish troops who had come to assassinate the prince while he slept.

Subject: a pug
Verb: saved
Object: the life

Simple version: <u>A pug saved the life of William the Silent.</u>

Trim the fat:

- The date at the beginning is set off by commas, so it is not necessary.
- The pug's name and William's title are extra descriptive information but non-essential.
- The second half of the sentence ("by barking … while he slept") is more information about just how the pug managed to save the prince's life, but we understand the main idea without those details.

But don't trim:

- We need to know whose life the pug saved, so keep "of William the Silent."

8. Anakin's first prosthesis, which was a replacement for the right arm he lost in a fight with Dooku, was connected to his body by a synthennet neural interface, which allowed him to register feeling in the mechanical limb.

    Subject: Anakin's prosthesis
    Verb: was connected
    Object: to his body

    Simple version: <u>Anakin's prosthesis was connected to his body by an interface.</u>

    Trim the fat:

    *   There are not one but *two* phrases that start with *which* in this sentence. They can both be cut.
    *   *First* is an extra adjective, so it can be ignored.
    *   Technical terms ("synthennet neural") are just like extra adjectives, so they can also be ignored.

    But don't trim:

    *   The phrase "by an interface" is a lot easier to understand once we got rid of the "synthennet neural" part of it, and it tells us how the prosthesis was attached, which is probably an important detail. Keep it.

SUMMARY

1. "Trim the fat" in a sentence to get at the meat, or the main idea.
2. Parts of a sentence that can usually be cut include
    *   Phrases that start with the word *which*
    *   Adjectives and descriptive phrases that provide details but aren't essential to the main parts of a sentence
    *   Phrases set off from the rest of the sentence by commas, whether at the beginning, in the middle, or at the end of a sentence
    *   Most prepositional phrases
    *   Technical terms and sometimes proper nouns

BUT WHAT DOES THAT WORD MEAN?

Remember this example?

Original version:

> *The mercurial, tawny fox bounds over the indolent canine.*

Simple version:

> *The … fox … bounds over the … canine.*

All the fat cut from the very first sentence we looked at was difficult vocabulary. Let's look at another example with tougher vocabulary.

> *Because of the manifold, scabrous details divulged in the publicity surrounding her divorce proceedings, the movie star became the target of much scurrilous gossip in the blogosphere.*

Now that you are a pro at cutting the fat, you may be thinking "there is an extra descriptive phrase at the beginning of this sentence that is unnecessary!" You are absolutely right, so cut it. We are left with the following:

> *The movie star became the target of much scurrilous gossip in the blogosphere.*

Now we can focus on our three main parts and cut out any remaining extra fat, which leaves us with

Yuganov Konstantin/Shutterstock.com

> *The movie star became the target of gossip.*

The extra words we cut, whether they were tough vocabulary or not, add detail, but they are not essential to understanding the general idea of the sentence.

Sometimes, however, the hard vocabulary is one of the three important parts of the sentence, in which case cutting the fat is not as useful. Here is an example.

> *The proletarians, angered by the death of Rue, the young tribute from their district, destroyed the screen broadcasting the games before the Peace Keepers arrived.*

First, trim some unnecessary descriptive phrases that are set off from the rest of the sentence with commas. That leaves us with the following:

> *The proletarians destroyed the screen broadcasting the games before the Peace Keepers arrived.*

Now we can focus on the main parts. The verb is *destroyed*, and the subject is *proletarians*—a difficult vocabulary word. However, from the verb *destroyed* and the object *screen* we can tell that *proletarians* must mean people of some kind. Therefore, we can simply replace the word *proletarians* with *people* to get a general understanding of the sentence.

> *The people destroyed the screen.*

Once you get the general idea, you can go back and fill in more details if you need them. In this example, the descriptive phrases we cut the first time through give us some clues about what kind of people the proletarians are—we know they are people from Rue's district.

This technique also works when the difficult vocabulary is a verb. Here is another example.

> *After the previous rebellion, the Capitol had subjugated the outlying districts by establishing the Hunger Games, which it claimed were meant to provide entertainment, but in reality, they helped to keep rebellions in check.*

Start again by cutting the extra descriptive phrases, and we have

> *The Capitol had subjugated the outlying districts.*

Replace the difficult vocabulary word with a simple phrase, and we come up with the following:

> *The Capitol did something to the outlying districts.*

Now that we have the general idea, we can go back to the descriptions we cut earlier to see that the thing the Capitol did was to keep rebellions in check.

Practice: Difficult Vocabulary

The following sentences contain one or more difficult vocabulary words. Instead of focusing on what you may not know, start by cutting the fat. Then simplify each sentence by replacing difficult words with more familiar ones whenever possible. Check your answers at the end of this practice exercise.

1. The provenance of the sonnet "To the Supreme Being," typically attributed to Michelangelo, and famously rendered in English by Wordsworth, has been challenged by some scholars.

   Trim the fat:

   _____

   _____

   Simplify:

   _____

   _____

2. Though the repeal of the Glass–Steagall Act in 1999 did not engender excessive controversy, in the wake of the 2008 financial crisis, some members of Congress are now pushing to resuscitate the legislation, which was originally passed in 1933 to separate traditional banks from the riskier financial services industry.

   Trim the fat:

   _____

   _____

   Simplify:

   _____

   _____

3. The Austrian music theorist Heinrich Shenker is most famous for having devised the eponymous mode of musical analysis based on the concepts of tonal space and primal structure.

Dmitrydesign/Shutterstock.com

Trim the fat:

_____

_____

Simplify:

_____

_____

4. In oxygenic photosynthesis, water furnishes the requisite electrons for the reduction reaction that converts carbon dioxide into a carbohydrate, and this hydrolysis also yields oxygen.

Trim the fat:

_____

_____

davidundderriese/Shutterstock.com

Simplify:

_____

_____

5. Although opera as we know it today began with Jacopo Peri's *Dafne*, this seminal work was not an exercise in innovation, but rather an attempt to revive classical Greek drama.

Trim the fat:

_____

_____

Simplify:

_____

_____

6. William Perkin unwittingly produced mauve, the first synthetic dye, while trying to engineer artificial quinine in his endeavor to cure malaria.

Trim the fat:

_____

_____

Simplify:

_____

_____

Answers and Explanations: Difficult Vocabulary

If you didn't simplify as much as the explanations here do, good for you—that means you have great vocabulary! Nevertheless, don't be afraid to replace touch vocabulary words with something really generic so that you can get the big picture in a sentence.

1. The provenance of the sonnet "To the Supreme Being," typically attributed to Michelangelo and famously rendered in English by Wordsworth, has been challenged by some scholars.

   Trim the fat: <u>The provenance has been challenged.</u>
   - Cut out the prepositional phrase "of the sonnet. . . ."
   - The descriptive phrases in the middle that are set off by commas can also be cut.

   Simplify: <u>Something has been challenged.</u>
   - Replace *provenance*, a tough word, with *something* to arrive at the general meaning.

2. Though the repeal of the Glass–Steagall Act in 1999 did not engender excessive controversy, in the wake of the 2008 financial crisis, some members of Congress are now pushing to resuscitate the legislation, which was originally passed in 1933 to separate traditional banks from the riskier financial services industry.

   Trim the fat: <u>Members of Congress are pushing to resuscitate the legislation.</u>
   - Cut the two descriptive phrases at the beginning of the sentence and the phrase starting with *which* at the end. This gets rid of a lot of the hard vocabulary that might otherwise make the sentence hard to understand.
   - Extra adjectives, such as *some* and *now*, can also be cut.

   Simplify: <u>Members of Congress are doing something to the legislation.</u>
   - If "pushing to resuscitate" seems confusing, just replace it with "doing something."

3. The Austrian music theorist Heinrich Shenker is most famous for having devised the eponymous mode of musical analysis based on the concepts of tonal space and primal structure.

    Trim the fat: <u>The music theorist is most famous for having devised the mode of musical analysis.</u>

    - The proper name and nationality of the theorist aren't the most important details, so cut them.
    - Take out the difficult adjective *eponymous* as well as the description of what the analysis is based on.

    Simplify: <u>A guy is famous for having done something with an analysis.</u>

    - If you don't know what a music theorist is, no problem. It's obviously a person—replace it with *a guy*.
    - Similarly, if you're unsure what *devised* means, you know it's a verb, so make it simpler.

4. In oxygenic photosynthesis, water furnishes the requisite electrons for the reduction reaction that converts carbon dioxide into a carbohydrate, and this hydrolysis also yields oxygen.

    Trim the fat: <u>Water furnishes electrons for the reaction that converts carbon dioxide into a carbohydrate.</u>

    - Cut out the descriptive phrase at the beginning that's set off from the rest of the sentence by a comma, as well as the phrase at the end, also set off by a comma.
    - Getting rid of the two extra phrases gets rid of a lot of the hard, sciency jargon in this sentence, but we can also eliminate the extra adjectives *requisite* and *reduction*.

    Simplify: <u>Water does something for the reaction that converts one thing into another thing.</u>

    - Get rid of the rest of the hard, sciency vocabulary by replacing it with the easier-to-understand *does something* for the verb and *thing* and *another thing* for the nouns.

5. Although opera as we know it today began with Jacopo Peri's *Dafne*, this seminal work was not an exercise in innovation, but rather an attempt to revive classical Greek drama.

   Trim the fat: This seminal work was not an exercise in innovation, but rather an attempt to revive classical Greek drama.

   - Cut out the descriptive phrase at the beginning of the sentence.

   Simplify: A thing was an attempt to revive something.

   - *Seminal work*? Huh? Staring at it isn't going to make it easier to understand. It's the subject, so just replace it with *thing*.
   - It matters a lot more what the thing was, not what it wasn't, so we can cut out everything from *not* up to *an attempt*.
   - Not sure exactly what classical Greek drama is? Again, simplify. Make it *something*.

6. William Perkin unwittingly produced mauve, the first synthetic dye, while trying to engineer artificial quinine in his endeavor to cure malaria.

   Trim the fat: William Perkin produced mauve while trying to engineer artificial quinine.

   - Cut out the difficult descriptive word *unwittingly*.
   - Ignore the descriptive phrase after *mauve*.
   - The prepositional phrase starting with *in* that closes the sentence can also go.

   Simplify: A guy produced something while trying to do something else.

   - Don't focus on not knowing who William Perkin is—he's a guy.
   - It's not a problem if you don't know exactly what *mauve* and *quinine* are; it's good enough to know that they're different, and the one William Perkin ended up with wasn't the one he set out to make.

SUMMARY

When dealing with difficult vocabulary, focus on what you do know rather than what you don't know.

- Start by trimming the fat, especially hard adjectives and descriptive phrases with lots of tough vocabulary.

- When you're left with important parts of the sentence that still have difficult vocabulary, identify which part it is (or they are), and replace hard words with easier versions. Most verbs can be replaced with a version of *does something*, and nouns can be replaced with *a person, a place*, or *a thing*.

WHAT ABOUT THE DETAILS?

In a few of the sentences in the last drill, we cut out almost every detail except the generic versions of the subject, verb, and object. That works for getting a very basic idea of what the sentence says, but what happens when you have to make sense of a difficult sentence in order to answer a question about it on a test? Put some details back in once you get the main idea.

Take a look at one of the examples from the last section again.

> *After the previous rebellion, the Capitol had subjugated the outlying districts by establishing the Hunger Games, which it claimed were meant to provide entertainment, but in reality, they helped to keep rebellions in check.*

Here is the simplified version.

> *The Capitol did something to the outlying districts.*

Let's look at how we can use clues in the sentence to help us figure out what "did something" means. First, the descriptive phrase that we cut from the beginning of the sentence tells us that this thing the Capitol did was done "after the previous rebellion," so it was probably in some way related to that. Next, we can look at the extra descriptive phrases at the end of the sentence. First, the prepositional phrase "by establishing the Hunger Games," tells us *how* the Capitol did the thing it did. Next, the phrase starting with "which" tells us more about *why* the Capitol did it. The Capitol *claimed* the Games "were meant to provide entertainment," but we already know from the beginning that they probably had something to do with the rebellion. And the next word, *but*, tells us that entertainment was not the real purpose. The true reason was "to keep rebellions in check." So "did something" means the Capitol kept the rebellions in check, and we can add this detail back to the original sentence.

> *The Capitol kept rebellions in check in the outlying districts.*

If you have already read *The Hunger Games*, and you know what happened, that sentence probably does not seem so tough. But what if you run into a sentence on a topic you know nothing about? Remember this one?

> *Although opera as we know it today began with Jacopo Peri's Dafne, this seminal work was not an exercise in innovation, but rather an attempt to revive classical Greek drama.*

Here is the simplified version.

> *A thing was an attempt to revive something.*

This version tells us very little, so let's see whether we can figure out what some of the tough vocabulary that we replaced with the generic words *thing* and *something* means.

The subject in the original sentence was "this seminal work," which we replaced with "a thing." Instead of focusing on how you *don't* know what that means, focus on what you *do* know. The word "this" before the tough vocabulary tells us that "seminal work" refers to something that was just discussed. The thing that was just discussed is "Jacopo Peri's *Dafne*," so now we know what the "seminal work" is. But, unless you are a hardcore classical music buff, that's probably not much help. So let's look at what else the sentence says about *Dafne*. The rest of that descriptive phrase we cut from the beginning of the sentence tells us that "opera as we know it today began with Jacopo Peri's *Dafne*." In other words, *Dafne* was the beginning of modern opera. Getting back to our original tough vocabulary, this tells us that "seminal" must mean something that comes at the beginning or starts something new.

Now we can add a little more detail to the simplified version of this sentence.

> *The first modern opera was an attempt to revive something.*

That might be enough information to help us answer a multiple-choice question about this sentence, but what if we needed to know more about the "something" that we used to replace "classical Greek drama?" Again, we can use other information in the sentence to figure out a little more about just what that is.

To begin with, the very first word in the original part of the sentence is "although." *Although* lets us know that the two parts of this sentence don't match each other. The first part told us that the subject, *Dafne*, was the first modern opera. We would expect something that was the first of its kind to do something new, right? Remember that part we cut out that told us what *Dafne* didn't do? It said that *Dafne* "was not an exercise in innovation." Just as the *although* at the beginning of the sentence led us to expect, the first modern opera **didn't** do something new. We know that it was an attempt to revive something, and if that wasn't something new, it must have been something old. Thus, classical Greek drama must be an old kind of drama.

Here is our new-and-improved, details-added simplified version of this sentence.

> *The first modern opera was an attempt to revive an old type of drama.*

Practice: Add the Details

Use the clues in the following sentences that you already simplified in the last drill to add some details back in. You can check your answers at the end of this practice section.

1. **Original:** *Though the repeal of the Glass–Steagall Act in 1999 did not engender excessive controversy, in the wake of the 2008 financial crisis, some members of Congress are now pushing to resuscitate the legislation, which was originally passed in 1933 to separate traditional banks from the riskier financial services industry.*

    Simplified: *Members of Congress are doing something to the legislation.*

    What does *doing something* mean?

    _____

    _____

    What is the *legislation* about?

    _____

    _____

    New sentence:

    _____

    _____

2. **Original:** *William Perkin unwittingly produced mauve, the first synthetic dye, while trying to engineer artificial quinine in his endeavor to cure malaria.*

   Simplified: *A guy produced something while trying to do something else.*

   What does *something* mean?

   _____

   _____

   What does *something else* mean?

   _____

   _____

   New sentence:

   _____

   _____

Answers and Explanations: Add the Details

1. **Original:** *Though the repeal of the Glass–Steagall Act in 1999 did not engender excessive controversy, in the wake of the 2008 financial crisis, some members of Congress are now pushing to resuscitate the legislation, which was originally passed in 1933 to separate traditional banks from the riskier financial services industry.*

   Simplified: *Members of Congress are doing something to the legislation.*

   What does *doing something* mean? <u>Bringing back.</u>

   The descriptive phrase at the beginning of this sentence tells us that the act was repealed in 1999. It also starts with *though*, which tells us that what comes later goes against the first part. There is another tough vocab word in there, *engender,* but focus on the easier words *not* and *controversy* instead. So the beginning tells us the repeal was not controversial, and we know because of the *though* at the beginning that what comes next will be different. If the repeal was not controversial at first, but now it is, what would members of Congress be doing? Probably the opposite of repeal, which would be to bring back.

   What is the *legislation* about? <u>Separating banking from financial services.</u>

   Just knowing the name of the legislation (the Glass–Steagall Act) is not all that helpful, but the phrase at the end of the sentence that starts with *which* tells us what it did.

   New sentence: <u>Members of Congress are pushing to bring back the legislation that separates banking from financial services.</u>

2. **Original:** *William Perkin unwittingly produced mauve, the first synthetic dye, while trying to engineer artificial quinine in his endeavor to cure malaria.*

   Simplified: *A guy produced something while trying to do something else.*

   What does *something* mean? <u>The first synthetic dye.</u>

   The information is in a descriptive phrase that we cut the first time through.

   What does *something else* mean? <u>Something that helps cure malaria.</u>

   The prepositional phrase that we cut tells us that artificial quinine, the tough vocabulary here, has something to do with curing malaria.

   New sentence: <u>A guy produced the first synthetic dye while trying to help cure malaria.</u>

SUMMARY

If you need more details, add them back in as needed after simplifying the sentence.

- Look at descriptive phrases and prepositional phrases, which will give you more information about tough vocabulary words.

- Look at conjunctions in a sentence that might give you a clue about whether the different parts say similar or different things. If one part of a sentence is easy to understand, a conjunction can help you make sense of the other part.

DEALING WITH PARAGRAPHS

Now that we have learned to pick apart the pieces of a tough sentence to better understand it, let's examine how we can use some of the same ideas to help us understand a tough paragraph. Here is an example.

> *The process of suburbanization that began in the second quarter of the nineteenth century was fundamentally linked to the nascence of the industrial city, and both of these advances were bound up with developments in transportation. Up until that time, the typical city had been a compact cluster of small buildings, which residents navigated primarily on foot; goods were moved by horse and cart. But as factories were built near waterways and rail stations on the outskirts of towns, more people arrived in the cities in search of work, which led to an increased demand for housing. As housing expanded around the factories, city borders expanded and better, more efficient transportation was developed to move people and goods around the newly enlarged cities.*

The first sentence of this paragraph is pretty hard to understand. Before going through the first part of this chapter, you might have just given up on it once you read the first sentence, but now you know better! Instead of giving up because you don't understand the first sentence, use the tools you learned earlier in this chapter. First, break it into two parts, then cut the fat and simplify.

> *A process was linked to something about industry. The process and the thing about industry were related to transportation.*

Like the opera example we looked at in the last section, this simplified version of the first sentence does not tell us a whole lot, but the rest of the paragraph can help us fill in the details.

Some of the sentences to which we added details in the last section had **transition** words that helped us figure out how the different parts of the sentences related to each other, and we want to be on the look out for the same kinds of words as we read through a paragraph. Conjunctions (such as *although, because, but*, and *and*) and time markers (such as *after, before,* and *since*) are especially important.

The second sentence of our paragraph begins with just such a time marker: "*up until that time.*" The first sentence mentioned a time, the second quarter of the nineteenth century, and this sentence will tell us what happened before that. But we also know that the process under discussion *started* at that time, so we can assume that the paragraph will go on to tell us about a change. See how much you can figure out just from a few words?

But let's get back to the details: *up until* things changed, the paragraph describes cities as compact places that people could easily walk around. Be on the lookout for those transition words, because they will indicate when the change took place. Sure enough, the next sentence starts with *but*, and then describes a change:

Factories were built on the edges of town, bringing more people, enlarging the cities, and leading to better transportation.

Now that we understand the details, we can answer the same detail questions we did in the last section. Let's start at the end here, with the *something about industry*. That must be the factories. So now we have

A process was linked to factories getting built on the edges of town.

What about the process? The thing that our paragraph describes happening after the factories were built was more people coming to the cities, making them larger. Add it in, along with the information about transportation.

Cities' growth was linked to factories getting built on the edges of town. Both the growth and the factories were related to better transportation.

By simplifying the topic sentence of this paragraph and then adding in details from the body of the paragraph, we did two things: made sense of the difficult first sentence **and** paraphrased the whole paragraph. It's no accident that we did both of these things because that is exactly how a well-written paragraph works: The topic sentence introduces an idea, and the body of the paragraph adds detail. In harder reading passages on standardized tests, usually either the topic sentence or the details are easier to understand. Focusing on the easier part, whichever one it is, can help you make sense of the harder part.

Transitions

Before we get to the drill on paragraphs, let's talk a little bit more about the transition words we've been talking about. Navigating through a difficult paragraph can be made much easier by paying close attention to the words that tell you how ideas are related to each other. There are five main types of these words to watch out for.

Opposite Direction

The following words indicate that ideas are unrelated to each other or the opposite of what we expect:

but	*although*	*even though*
yet	*instead*	*despite*
however	*nevertheless*	*in contrast*

Same Direction

These words indicate that ideas are related or that the author is giving additional explanation of an idea.

furthermore   *also*

additionally   *moreover*

Certain types of punctuation can also be same-direction transitions.

;   :

Conclusions

These words tell you that the author is about to sum up the main point. If what comes before one of these words is hard to understand, focus instead on what comes after it.

therefore   *so*

thus   *consequently*

Examples

A very common way to structure a paragraph is to make a claim and then use an example to support it. If you have trouble making sense of the claim part, understanding the example is usually helpful. The following words indicate that an example is coming:

for example   *in this case*

because   *similarly*

since

Time Indicators

Words that order events in time usually indicate change, as we saw in our last example. Watch out for words like these.

before   *until*

after   *since*

Practice: Paragraphs

Write a summary of each paragraph. Start by identifying a topic sentence. If it's difficult to understand, use your simplifying tools. Pay particular attention to transition words to help you figure out how ideas are related to each other, then add details from the body sentences to your final summary. You can check your answers at the end of this practice exercise.

1. Despite rampant gender bias in the burgeoning field of aviation early in the twentieth century, some women found ways to compete and even to triumph. Ruth Law, for example, set a new nonstop distance record in 1916 by flying 590 miles from Chicago to Hornell, New York. She was so successful that in 1917 she was earning as much as $9,000 per week for exhibition and stunt flights. Her success exemplified the resourcefulness and fortitude demanded of a woman who wanted to enter a male-dominated discipline.

    What does the topic sentence say?

    _____

    _____

    What are the transition words in the paragraph?

    _____

    _____

    Final summary:

    _____

    _____

    _____

2. According to traditional beliefs of the Hopi and Pueblo tribes, kachina, the spirits of dead ancestors, visit their villages on the winter solstice. Each kachina is said to possess both a specific personality and a lesson to impart to the members of the village. Many of the kachina play traditional roles. For instance, a chief brings lessons of wisdom, a mother brings lessons of love and patience, or an ogre teaches about discipline and behavior. However, there are also clown-like characters who act in outrageous ways during otherwise solemn ceremonies to bring comic relief. But this is not their only function; by breaking various taboos and transgressing boundaries set up by society, these clown characters provide examples to the younger members of the tribe of unacceptable conduct.

What does the topic sentence say?

_____

_____

What are the transition words in the paragraph?

_____

_____

Final summary:

_____

_____

_____

_____

3. The remarkable variety of geothermal features in Yellowstone National Park is the result of an ancient volcanic eruption, which created one of the largest known calderas. Although there is no longer an active volcano in Yellowstone, a shallow body of magma is responsible for the impressive geysers, hot springs, mud pots, and fumaroles. As cold water percolates through the permeable ground rock, it comes into contact with magma-heated brine, and is itself heated to well above the boiling point. Pressure, however, keeps this super-heated water from turning into steam. Because the resulting difference in density between the super-heated water and the cold water around it creates convection currents, the hot water is sent up to the surface through cracks in the rhyolitic lava flows, creating the iconic features of the park.

What does the topic sentence say?

_____

_____

What are the transition words in the paragraph?

_____

_____

Final summary:

_____

_____

_____

_____

4. By the early years of the nineteenth century, American landscape art was closely associated with the system of republican ideals of the new nation. It had become a potent force in the popular imagination because landscape painters used images to suggest limitless possibilities, which resonated with the view of America as occupying a unique role in world history. In other words, images of the American landscape became symbols of national pride.

What does the topic sentence say?

_____

_____

What are the transition words in the paragraph?

_____

_____

Final summary:

_____

_____

_____

_____

5. Before the invention of the piano, the expressive possibilities available to composers were limited by the harpsichord's lack of dynamic range. In the early eighteenth century, Bartolomeo Cristofori successfully built an instrument that was loud enough for large public performances and also allowed for expressive control of volume and sustained notes. Consequently, a new era in composition was ushered in with the greatly expanded expressive possibilities of Cristofori's design.

What does the topic sentence say?

_____

_____

What are the transition words in the paragraph?

_____

_____

Final summary:

_____

_____

_____

_____

Answers and Explanations: Paragraphs

1. *Despite rampant gender bias in the burgeoning field of aviation early in the twentieth century, some women found ways to compete and even to triumph. Ruth Law, for example, set a new nonstop distance record in 1916 by flying 590 miles from Chicago to Hornell, New York. She was so successful that in 1917 she was earning as much as $9,000 per week for exhibition and stunt flights. Her success exemplified the resourcefulness and fortitude demanded of a woman who wanted to enter a male-dominated discipline.*

   What does the topic sentence say? *Some women found ways to compete.*

   To get at the general meaning of the first sentence, we can ignore the whole first phrase starting with *despite*; we will add the details back in later.

   What are the transition words in the paragraph? *Despite, for example*

   Despite tells us that the first part of the topic sentence is different from the second part. Cut out some extra adjectives, and the sentence tells us there was gender bias in aviation.

   For example lets us know that we are going to read about a situation that illustrates the idea we just read about. Without even reading past this transition, we know that Ruth Law was a successful pilot. Sure enough, the next few sentences go on to tell us about her success.

   Final summary: *Despite gender bias in aviation, some women, including Ruth law, were successful pilots.*

2. *According to traditional beliefs of the Hopi and Pueblo tribes, kachina, the spirits of dead ancestors, visit their villages on the winter solstice. Each kachina is said to possess both a specific personality and a lesson to impart to the members of the village. Many of the kachina play traditional roles, teaching by example. For instance, a chief brings lessons of wisdom, a mother brings lessons of love and patience, or an ogre teaches about discipline and behavior. However, there are also clown-like characters that act in outrageous ways during otherwise solemn ceremonies to bring comic relief. But this is not their only function; by breaking various taboos and transgressing boundaries set up by society, these clown characters provide examples to the younger members of the tribe of unacceptable conduct.*

   What does the topic sentence say? *The spirits of dead ancestors visit villages.*

   The beginning phrase of the first sentence can be cut. If you don't know what a *kachina* is, no problem—the sentence explains it for you.

What are the transition words in the paragraph? *For instance, however, but, ;*

The first transition, *for instance*, shows up several sentences after the first sentence of the paragraph. *For instance* indicates an example is coming, and the sentences before that give us some more information about what the example is about: The spirits have personalities and teach lessons, many of which are traditional. Nothing too tough here. The examples that come after *for instance* give us some specific examples.

The next transition, *however*, tells us that the ideas are about to change. What have we just been reading about? Traditional lessons taught by spirits. What do we expect to read about next? Non-traditional lessons. The next example given is the clown spirits that provide comic relief. This certainly seems different from the examples that came before the *however*.

But the paragraph is not over yet—our next transition is *but*, indicating another shift in ideas, and immediately after that, we see that comic relief is not the only thing these clown spirits do.

The final transition is a semicolon, which indicates that the second part of this sentence agrees with the first part. Good thing we know that much, because the rest of this sentence has some harder vocabulary. This is a great example of the details being harder to understand than the main idea. As always, though, we can focus on what we *do* know and understand. If we do some simplifying and cutting, the basic idea here is that by doing something the clowns provide examples of unacceptable conduct. This makes perfect sense in relation to the rest of the paragraph—remember the original *however*, which made us think we were going to read about non-traditional lessons? Here is the example of that. Even if you don't understand exactly what the *something* the clowns do is, you know *why* they do it.

Final summary: *The spirits of dead ancestors visit villages to teach lessons. Most of them teach by example, but some teach by showing what not to do.*

3.   *The remarkable variety of geothermal features in Yellowstone National Park is the result of an ancient volcanic eruption, which created one of the largest-known calderas. Although there is no longer an active volcano in Yellowstone, a shallow body of magma is responsible for the impressive geysers, hot springs, mud pots, and fumaroles. As cold water percolates through the permeable ground rock, it comes into contact with magma-heated brine, and is itself heated to well above the boiling point. Pressure, however, keeps this super-heated water from turning into steam. Because the resulting difference in density between the super-heated water and*

the cold water around it creates convection currents, the hot water is sent up to the surface through cracks in the rhyolitic lava flows, creating the iconic features of the park.

What does the topic sentence say? *The features in Yellowstone are the result of a volcanic eruption.*

There are several extra adjectives as well as a *which* phrase at the end of the sentence that we can cut. Some of these words are harder vocabulary, and cutting them makes the sentence easier to understand.

What are the transition words in the paragraph? *Although, however, because*

Following the first transition word, *although*, we find out that there is not an active volcano in Yellowstone. We also know from the *although* that the second part of the sentence will tell us something different. There are a bunch of words in the second part of this paragraph that might be unfamiliar, but we can simplify them: Something is responsible for something else. The beginning told us that volcanoes are no longer active, and because we know the second part is different, the first *something* is probably related to volcanoes. As for the second *something*, lists are usually related items, so pick out one that you understand: Something volcanic causes hot springs. See how this is more or less a restating of the first sentence?

The next sentence begins a description of how this process happens. Again, there are some vocabulary words that may be unfamiliar, but focus on what you do know and simplify when necessary: As cold water goes through the ground, it touches something hot and is heated.

Then comes our next transition, *however, which* introduces a sentence that explains why the water does not turn into steam, as we would expect it to, when it gets heated.

The final transition, *because*, lets us know that the ideas in the last two sentences are connected and that one causes the other. Again, simplify the harder jargon: The difference in density creates currents that send the hot water to the surface.

Final summary: *Although there is no longer an active volcano in Yellowstone, something volcanic causes the hot springs. Cold water goes through the ground, is heated, and a difference in density sends the hot water back to the surface.*

The second sentence of this paragraph says almost the same thing as the first, the topic sentence. There's no need to include the same idea twice in a summary, so just start with the second sentence.

4. *By the early years of the nineteenth century, American landscape art was closely associated with the system of republican ideals of the new nation. It had become a potent force in the popular imagination because landscape painters used images to suggest limitless possibilities, which resonated with the view of America as occupying a unique role in world history. In other words, images of the American landscape became symbols of national pride.*

What does the topic sentence say? *American landscape art was closely associated with the ideals of the new nation.*

Cut the description at the beginning and some extra descriptive words to get the main idea.

What are the transition words in the paragraph? *In other words*

Because there is no transition between the first and second sentences of the paragraph, we know that the second sentence gives more detail or explanation about the first one. Good thing we know that much, because the second sentence is pretty hard to follow.

There is no need to simplify the second sentence, however, because the third sentence starts with the phrase *in other words*, which tells you that the author is about to say the same idea in different words. Luckily, this sentence is much easier to understand.

Final summary: *American landscape art was closely associated with the ideals of the new nation. Images of the landscape became symbols of national pride.*

5. *Before the invention of the piano, the expressive possibilities available to composers were limited by the harpsichord's lack of dynamic range. In the early eighteenth century, Bartolomeo Cristofori successfully built an instrument that was loud enough for large public performances and also allowed for expressive control of volume and sustained notes. Consequently, a new era in composition was ushered in with the greatly expanded expressive possibilities of Cristofori's design.*

What does the topic sentence say? *Before the invention of the piano, expression was limited.*

Most of the extra information here is prepositional phrases. Get rid of them to arrive at the general idea of the sentence.

What are the transition words in the paragraph? *Before, consequently*

The word *before* right at the beginning of the sentence is a time indicator, which tells us that something changed. The topic sentence lets us know that the old way was limited expression. So we expect the next part to tell us about a change that came with the invention of the piano, and that's exactly what the second sentence does. If we simplify the second sentence, it tells us that a guy built an instrument that was loud and allowed for expressive control. What was the instrument? The topic sentence tells us it was the piano. Who is Bartolomeo Cristofori? The guy who invented the piano.

The next transition word, *consequently*, tells us the result of this new invention: a new era in composition.

Final summary: *Before the invention of the piano, expression was limited. The piano was loud and allowed for expressive control, and as a result a new era in composition began.*

SUMMARY

The big idea here is the same as in the last section: When dealing with difficult paragraphs, focus on what you do know rather that what you don't know.

- Simplify the topic sentence of a paragraph first, to get the main idea.

- Focus on transition words to help you figure out the relationships between ideas in the paragraph.

- Fill in details as necessary to understand the specifics of the paragraph.

PUTTING IT ALL TOGETHER

On a standardized test, we usually have a whole passage to read, not just single paragraphs. Moreover, we have to answer questions about the passage, not just summarize it. Let's look at how we can put all the tools we've learned so far together to make sense of a tough passage and answer the questions that go with it.

A passage is made of paragraphs, so let's use the first tool we used on paragraphs to help make sense of a whole passage: Look at the topic sentence first. In the following passage, we'll read just the topic sentences and see how much we can learn from them:

[1]

Until a few decades ago, lunar geologists generally believed that the craters on the moon were the product of volcanic activity. Blah blah blah blah blah. Blah blah blah. Blah, blah blah, blah blah.

[2]

But further study suggests that craters on the moon cannot be explained the same way. Blah blah blah blah blah. Blah blah. Blah. Blah blah blah blah blah. Blah blah blah blah blah blah blah blah blah blah blah.

[3]

Despite these differences, there is a remarkable similarity between these lunar craters and a particular crater in Arizona, which is unusual in that it originated not from volcanic activity, but rather from the impact of a meteorite. Blah blah blah blah blah. Blah blah blah. Blah blah blah blah blah. Blah blah blah blah blah blah blah blah blah blah blah. Blah blah blah blah.

[4]

The moon is host to legions of craters parallel to the one in Arizona, and researchers now believe that they were produced by similar collisions. Blah blah blah blah blah. Blah blah blah. Blah blah blah, blah blah.

[5]

The largest lunar craters originate from impacts with meteorites much larger than the one that struck Arizona. Blah blah blah blah blah. Blah blah blah. Blah blah blah blah blah. Blah blah blah blah blah. Blah blah blah blah blah blah.

The collision of an object of this size with Earth would have dramatic consequences for the entire planet and all life on it. Blah blah blah blah blah. Blah blah blah. Blah blah blah blah blah. Blah blah blah blah blah blah blah blah blah blah blah blah. Blah blah blah blah blah. Blabbety blah blah blah.

7

Even after the immediate effects of the strike had subsided, smoke and dust in the atmosphere would have blotted out the Sun and dramatically lowered temperatures over the following weeks. Blah blah blah blah blah. Blah blah blah. Blah blah blah blah blah. Blah blah blah blah blah. Blah blah blah blah blah blah blah.

You can learn a lot about a passage just by reading its topic sentences. Let's look at the first sentence of the first paragraph.

> *Until a few decades ago, lunar geologists generally believed that the craters on the moon were the product of volcanic activity.*

It starts out with a time transition: *Until a few decades ago.* Just by reading those first five words, we know that we're going to read about a change. The rest of the sentence tells us what the old idea was: Geologists thought craters on the moon were made by volcanoes. But because the time transition indicated that there's a change coming, we know that volcanoes didn't make the craters. When we continue reading, we should be on the lookout for what the new idea is.

Now let's look at the beginning of the second paragraph.

> *But further study suggests that craters on the moon cannot be explained the same way.*

Just as we suspected—the old idea was wrong.

But that's not all this sentence tells us! It both confirms what we already knew about the first paragraph, that it was about the old idea, and lets us know that this paragraph will be about the new idea.

Now we're ready to tackle the third paragraph.

> *Despite these differences, there is a remarkable similarity between these lunar craters and a particular crater in Arizona, which is unusual in that it originated not from volcanic activity, but rather from the impact of a meteorite.*

Again, this paragraph starts with a transition: *despite these differences*. That lets us know that the previous paragraph must have told us about some differences. And we already know what the differences have to do with: the old, wrong, idea about the craters and the new idea. More specifically, because we know what the old, wrong idea is, the differences are probably between volcanic craters and moon craters. But the word *despite* tells us that we are about to read about something that is *not* different.

Sure enough, the next part of the sentence mentions a *similarity*. The similarity is between the craters on the moon and a crater in Arizona. The last part of the sentence, the phrase starting with *which*, gives us more information about this one crater in Arizona. First, it tells us that it's *unusual*. That goes along with everything else we've read so far, which has indicated change and difference. Second, we find out that this crater in Arizona was made by a meteorite, not a volcano.

Do you have any thoughts yet about where the moon craters came from? Remember, they were not made by volcanoes, so perhaps they were made by meteorites.

Here is the first sentence of the fourth paragraph.

> *The moon is host to legions of craters congruent to the one in Arizona, and researchers now believe that they were produced by similar collisions.*

This sentence is harder to follow than the previous three, but remember your tools, focus on what you can understand, and let's see what sense we can make of it. The second part, after the *and,* has easier vocabulary than the first part. Because *and* tells us that the two parts agree with each other, let's start with the second part of the sentence. It says *researchers now believe*, so we are finally going to hear what that new idea is! The new idea is *that they were produced by similar collisions*. What are *they*? If we look back at the first part of the sentence, focusing on what we can understand, we see that *they* are moon craters.

Remember the prediction we made about the new idea that the moon craters were made by meteorites? Here is our confirmation of that prediction—the moon craters were made by *similar collisions*. Similar to what? Similar to the *impact of a meteorite* mentioned in the third paragraph.

Before moving on to the fifth paragraph, let's take a moment to recap what we know so far.

- Geologists used to think craters on the moon were made by volcanoes.
- But they don't think that anymore.
- There's one crater in Arizona that was made by a meteorite that is similar to the moon craters.
- The new idea about the moon craters is that they were also made by meteorites.

Now let's examine the first sentence of the fifth paragraph.

> *The largest lunar craters originated from impacts with meteorites much larger than the one that struck Arizona.*

Unlike all the rest of the topic sentences we have looked at so far, there is no transition in this one. No transitions indicate that there's no change in direction; in other words, this paragraph continues on in the same vein as the last paragraph, which was about how collisions with meteorites made the moon craters. This paragraph goes into more detail, telling us about the *largest* of the craters and the size of the meteorites that made them.

Moving on to the beginning of the sixth paragraph.

> *The collision of an object of this size with Earth would have monumental consequences for the entire planet and all life on it.*

Again, there are no transitions in this sentence. It mentions *an object of this size*, which lets us know that the previous paragraph probably went on to talk in more detail about the large meteorites. This sentence introduces a new idea about impacts with meteorites, which is the possibility of a large meteorite hitting Earth. The topic sentence here tells us there would be big consequences for life on Earth if that were to happen, so what do you think the rest of the paragraph will discuss? It will probably address what those consequences would be.

Now let's look at the topic sentence of the final paragraph.

> *Even after the immediate effects of the strike had subsided, smoke and dust in the atmosphere would have blotted out the Sun and dramatically lowered temperatures over the following weeks.*

Finally, we have another transition: *even after*, which is a same direction transition; it tells us that there is no change here. We thought the previous paragraph was going to describe the consequences of a large meteorite hitting Earth, and this sentence confirms that idea because it refers to after the *immediate effects*. And when we read the second part of the sentence, it matches what the transition led us to expect: More bad stuff would happen as time went on.

Here's our final summary of the passage, just based on what we learned from the topic sentences.

- Geologists used to think craters on the moon were made by volcanoes.
- But they don't think that anymore, because moon craters are different from volcanic craters.
- There's one crater in Arizona similar to the moon craters that was made by a meteorite.
- The new idea bout the moon craters is that they were also made by meteorites.
- Big craters on the moon were made by really big meteorites.
- If a really big meteorite hit Earth, it would have a big effect on all life.
- Both the immediate and the long-term effects would be bad.

Now that we have an introduction to this passage based on the topic sentences, let's see how that can help us answer questions. Here's the whole passage, plus five questions about it like you would see on a standardized test. There's no need to read the whole passage before attacking the questions; we already have a pretty good idea of what it's about. Go straight to the first question, and we'll refer back to the passage as necessary to answer the questions.

This passage is adapted from the article "Who Moved My Cheese?: The Real Story of Lunar Craters" by John Spencer (© 2005 *Astronomy Today*).

Until a few decades ago, lunar geologists generally believed that the craters on the moon were the product of volcanic activity. Craters of the Moon National Monument, in
Line southeastern Idaho, is a prime exemplar of this belief: it was
5 so named in the early twentieth century because the ostensibly barren, volcanic terrain was perceived to be a terrestrial manifestation of the lunar landscape.

But further study suggests that craters on the moon cannot be explained the same way. The key divergence
10 between terrestrial and lunar craters is in their contour. Craters on Earth are usually a sharply conoidal shape with a comparatively small concavity on the top, as we might expect of landforms produced by volcanoes. Conversely, a lunar crater more closely approximates a sports stadium. Its characteristic
15 shape is a plateau-like center enclosed by tiered rings culminating at the crater's rim.

Despite these differences, there is a remarkable similarity between these lunar craters and a particular crater in Arizona, which is unusual in that it originated not from volcanic
20 activity, but rather from the impact of a meteorite. Imagine a massive piece of rock, large enough to survive entering Earth's atmosphere, traveling at a velocity of about 10 miles per second. Such an object would release a formidable amount of heat when it made impact, and the meteorite and the circumforaneous
25 earth would dissolve. It would also, like a stone striking the surface of a pond, catapult liquefied material upward and outward in a large circle. By measuring the dimensions of the Arizona crater, scientists have determined that the impactor must have weighed about 200,000 tons and had a diameter of
30 about 100 feet.

The moon is host to legions of craters congruent to the one in Arizona, and researchers now believe that they were produced by similar collisions. The moon's lack of atmosphere means that meteorites of diverse sizes collide with the lunar
35 surface, and its lack of plate tectonics and weather ensure that the ensuing craters do not erode. This means that the lunar craters endure indefinitely, and are readily available for researchers to study.

The largest lunar craters originated from impacts with
40 meteorites much larger than the one that struck Arizona. Clavius, which measures in at an impressive 146 miles in diameter and is one of the largest of the lunar craters, must have been formed by an impactor of at least 200 billion

tons. Such a meteorite would be approximately four miles in
45 diameter, comparable to a sizeable mountain on Earth.

The collision of an object of this size with Earth would have
monumental consequences for the entire planet and all life on
it. In fact, scientists now believe that a larger meteorite (six
miles in diameter) actually did strike the Earth 65 million
50 years ago. This collision created the recently discovered
Chicxulub crater buried deep within the Yucatan Peninsula
and the Gulf of Mexico. The Chicxulub crater measures 112
miles wide, and has only recently been discovered because it
lies in the crust of the earth below the ocean. When the impact
55 that produced this crater happened, an area the size of Europe
would have been almost instantaneously flattened and scoured
of virtually all life, and massive earthquakes and tsunamis
would have quickly followed. As the excavated material, ejected
out of Earth's atmosphere by the force of the impact, began
60 to rain back down on the planet, the heat generated by its re-
entry would have irradiated the Earth's surface, starting great
conflagrations that reduced most of the world's great forests
and grasslands to ash.

Even after the immediate effects of the strike had subsided,
65 smoke and dust in the atmosphere would have blotted out the
Sun and dramatically lowered temperatures over the following
weeks. Surviving plant life quickly would wilt and die, and
even most marine life would perish, killed by sulfur and other
poisons that spilled into the seas as a result of forest fires
70 and acid rain. Our ability to study the lunar craters via space
missions and powerful telescopes has helped us put together a
clear picture of the impact of this cataclysmic event on Earth 65
million years ago. Without the knowledge we have gained from
studying the craters on the moon, this giant crater under the
75 sea may never have been discovered, much less understood.

1. In terms of the effect it would have on life on Earth, the
   impact of a large meteorite is described by the author
   as:

   a) instantaneously flattening Europe.
   b) as massive as an earthquake and a tsunami.
   c) similar to a rock splashing in a pond.
   d) producing cataclysmic results including
      earthquakes, wildfires, and acid rain.

Step 1: Find the relevant part of the passage. From our initial read-through of
the topic sentences, we know that the discussion of a large meteorite hitting Earth
occurs briefly in the third paragraph—in relation to the crater in Arizona—and
then in more detail in the last two paragraphs. If we look more closely at exactly
what the question is asking, it specifies the *effect on life on Earth*, which is what the
sixth paragraph is about, and the seventh paragraph continues the discussion.

Step 2: Read the relevant part of the passage. Read the whole sixth and seventh
paragraphs, using your cutting, simplifying, and detail-adding skills as necessary,
then see which answer choice best matches what you read.

Step 3: Use Process of Elimination (POE).

Choice (a) uses words from the passage that you probably remember reading, and that you're especially likely to remember reading if you're not trying to figure out what the passage is *actually* saying. But the answer takes those words, *instantaneously*, *flatten*, and *Europe*, and puts them together in the wrong way. The passage says "an area *the size of* Europe would have been almost instantaneously flattened," not that Europe itself was flattened. This kind of answer appears frequently on standardized tests, so let's call it "recycled language." *Eliminate choice (a).*

Choice (b) is also recycled language; the passage tells us that "massive earthquakes and tsunamis would have quickly followed," but the answer says that the impact would be "*as massive as* an earthquake and a tsunami." *Eliminate choice (b).*

Choice (c) does not appear anywhere in the sixth paragraph (in fact, it refers to something in the third paragraph, but as long as you know it's not in the part of the passage relevant to the question, you can still get rid of it). *Eliminate choice (c).*

Choice (d) tells us that the meteorite would *produce* earthquakes, wildfires, and acid rain, which matches the passage—earthquakes are mentioned in the sixth paragraph, and forest fires and acid rain in the seventh. We can use our simplifying tool with the answer choice to ignore the adjective "cataclysmic" at first if it's confusing. It's a good idea to double-check that it matches the passage. It appears toward the end of the seventh paragraph in the phrase *this cataclysmic event*. That refers to the large meteorite hitting Earth, so it also makes sense to use it to describe the effects of the event. ***Choice (d) is correct.***

2. Based on the passage, what relationship does the divergence described in the second paragraph (lines 8–16) have to the possibility that lunar craters are volcanic?

   a) It proves that Craters of the Moon National Monument is made of pieces of moon rock that collided with Earth.
   b) It suggests that lunar craters are formed a different way than volcanic craters are.
   c) It indicates that the plateau-like volcanic landforms found on Earth approximate lunar craters.
   d) It calls into question the theory that the sharply conoidal craters on the moon were formed by volcanoes.

Step 1: Find the relevant part of the passage. This question tells us exactly where to go—the second paragraph.

Step 2: Read the relevant part of the passage. Read the second paragraph, paying particular attention to the *divergence*, because that's what the question asks about. Remember what we already know about this paragraph: It tells us craters on the moon are not volcanic because they're different from craters on Earth. There's a description of craters on Earth in this paragraph, then a sentence that starts with *conversely*, which tells us that it's going to say something different. This sentence and the next describe what craters on the moon usually look like.

Step 3: POE

Choice (a) is recycled language, but not even language recycled from this paragraph. *Craters of the Moon National Monument* is in the first paragraph, and collisions with Earth are discussed later. *Eliminate choice (a).*

Choice (b) seems pretty good. Volcanic craters, we know from reading the topic sentences, are *not* what the lunar craters are. Be sure to check all four answer choices before making a final decision, though! *Don't eliminate choice (b).*

Choice (c) has some recycled language: *plateau-like* appears in this paragraph, but it describes craters on the moon, not "volcanic landforms on Earth." If something in an answer choice obviously contradicts the passage, you don't need to look at the rest of it. *Eliminate choice (c).*

Choice (d) tries the same trick that choice (c) does. This time, the phrases *conoidal craters* and *formed by volcanoes* are used to describe craters on the moon, but we know those are actually characteristics of craters on Earth. *Eliminate choice (d).*

Choice (b) is correct.

3. The main point of the first paragraph (lines 1–7) is that:

   a) scientists' theories about lunar craters have changed.
   b) Craters of the Moon National Monument was named for its similarity to the moon.
   c) lunar craters are a different shape than most terrestrial craters.
   d) the name of Craters of the Moon National Monument should be changed because its craters do not actually look like those on the moon.

Step 1: Find the relevant part of the passage. Again, this question tells you where to go in the passage—the first paragraph.

Step 2: Read the relevant part of the passage. Remember what we already know about the first paragraph: Geologists used to think that craters on the moon were formed by volcanoes, but they were wrong. The rest of the paragraph has some hard vocabulary, but the word *exemplar* indicates that Craters of the Moon National Monument is an example of the old idea. Therefore, the idea expressed in the topic sentence is the main point of the paragraph.

Step 3: POE

Choice (a) matches what we know about the first paragraph: Geologists' ideas about lunar craters have changed. *Don't eliminate choice (a)*, but we should still read all the other choices, just to be sure this one is the best choice.

Choice (b) matches what the passage says. According to the old idea described in the first paragraph, craters on the moon were similar to volcanic craters on Earth, and that's what gave the monument its name. But even if you didn't understand much of the paragraph, you know that the main point of the paragraph is that the old idea was that craters on the moon were formed by volcanoes, and the National Monument is an example of that. This choice is a detail of the paragraph, not its main point. *Eliminate choice (b)*.

Choice (c) refers to the second paragraph, not the first. *Eliminate choice (c)*.

Choice (d) is somewhat similar to choice (b), and also contains words out of context. Craters of the Moon National Monument is mentioned in the first paragraph, but is not the main point. The paragraph also doesn't say anything about *changing* its name. *Eliminate choice (d)*.

Choice (a) is correct.

4. Lines 23–27 mainly emphasize what quality?
   a) The effect of a stone striking the surface of a pond
   b) The temperature of a meteorite as it enters Earth's atmosphere
   c) The immediate physical results of a large meteorite colliding with the surface of Earth
   d) The characteristic shape of a crater formed by the impact of a meteorite on the surface of Earth

Step 1: Find the relevant part of the passage. Once again, the question directs you to a specific spot—part of the third paragraph.

Step 2: Read the relevant part of the passage. Read the whole third paragraph. We already know that it discusses a crater in Arizona that's similar to craters on the moon. The lines specified in the question tell us that a meteorite hitting Earth would be hot, and would act like a stone hitting the surface of a pond.

Step 3: POE

Choice (a) is in the passage. But the word *like* before the stone is mentioned indicates that it's a simile for the meteorite. The phrase *such an object* at the beginning of line 23 refers back to the meteorite. The description of the stone is there to illustrate what happened when the meteorite hit Earth. The impact of the meteorite is the main focus here, not the stone. *Eliminate choice (a).*

Choice (b) is also not the main focus. The passage tells us that the meteorite would be hot, but it's only part of a larger description. *Eliminate choice (b).*

Choice (c) is okay. *Immediate physical results*—this paragraph talks about "catapulting liquid material upward and outward." That seems pretty physical. *Don't eliminate choice (c)*, but be sure to check choice (d) before making a final decision.

Choice (d) refers to the wrong paragraph; *characteristic shape* refers to the second paragraph, not the third. The third paragraph talks about dimensions, but not shape. *Eliminate choice (d).*

Choice (c) is correct.

5. The author characterizes the similarity between lunar craters and sports stadiums as:
    a) proof that lunar craters are not volcanic and terrestrial craters are not formed by meteorites.
    b) evidence that a theory may be incorrect.
    c) a reason to start a football league on the moon.
    d) an indication that lunar craters are formed by meteorites.

Step 1: Find the relevant part of the passage. We know from answering question 2 that *sports stadiums* are part of the description of craters on the moon in the second paragraph.

Step 2: Read the relevant part of the passage. Review the second paragraph. Even if you don't understand all the words, use what you do know to understand what it says about sports stadiums. The third sentence describes the shape of craters on Earth and says that they are formed by volcanoes. The fourth sentence talks about lunar craters. We know from the transition *conversely* at the beginning of this sentence that the lunar craters are a different shape than craters on Earth. The words *more closely approximates* might be hard to understand, but we can reasonably assume that they describe the shape of craters on the moon, and the *sports stadium* is part of that description.

Step 3: POE

We know that this paragraph talks about the new idea, which is that craters on the moon are not formed by volcanoes.

Choice (a) matches that, but we haven't read anything about meteorites yet. The word *proof* is also very strong, and this paragraph tells us that *further study suggests*, which is not quite *proof. Eliminate choice (a).*

Choice (b) is closer: *evidence* better matches the sense of *further study suggests*. While the rest of the answer, *a theory may be incorrect*, is vague, there's nothing about it that contradicts what the second paragraph discusses. *Don't eliminate choice (b).*

Choice (c) comes out of nowhere. Sure, the passage mentions a sports stadium, but there's nothing about football, and *especially* nothing about football on the moon. *Eliminate choice (c).*

Choice (d) is similar to part of choice (a); we haven't read about meteorites yet. This paragraph tells us that the old idea is wrong, but hasn't yet told us what the new idea is. *Eliminate choice (d).*

Choice (b) is correct.

Practice: Putting It All Together

Here is another passage with questions for you to try. This time, start by reading the topic sentence of each paragraph. Simplify each sentence, and pay attention to transitions and what they tell you about what you should expect to read about in previous or subsequent paragraphs. Then answer the questions, going back to read more details as necessary. You can check your answers at the end of this practice exercise.

This passage is adapted from *The Life and Times of Harriet Beecher Stowe* by Anne T. Bellum (© 2002, University of Maine Press).

Although it has today largely fallen out of favor, *Uncle Tom's Cabin; or, Life Among the Lowly*, the anti-slavery novel written by abolitionist Harriet Beecher Stowe, was the best-selling

Line novel of the nineteenth century. In recent years, the novel has
5 been eschewed both because of its melodramatic, sentimental style and because of its role in establishing stereotypes of black characters. While modern tastes dictate that this influential novel is no longer a vital member of our literary canon, it retains historical importance as an instigator of the Civil War.

10 Stowe penned the novel, which was originally published as a 40-week serial that appeared from June, 1851 until April, 1852 in *The National Era*, in response to the expansion of the Fugitive Slave Law, passed by Congress in 1850, which greatly expanded the purview of the original 1793 legislation. Legal
15 punishment was broadened not only for runaway slaves and those who assisted them but also for those who declined to help capture runaways. Stowe was furious about the new law, and wrote in a letter to her sister, "I would write something that would make this whole nation feel what an accursed thing
20 slavery is."

The serial proved so popular that the publisher of *The National Era* had it printed in book form. Demand for its inaugural printing was so great that it promptly sold out and several more runs, in ever-more elaborate editions, were
25 printed within the first year. During that first year alone, 300,000 copies of the novel were sold in the United States, and 1.5 million copies made their ways into the hands of British readers. By 1857 *Uncle Tom's Cabin* had been translated into 20 languages.

30 Despite its world-wide popularity, *Uncle Tom's Cabin* did not escape controversy, even when it was first published. It comes as no surprise that the book was received with opprobrium in the South, and criticized for its lack of authenticity, as Stowe had never visited the South. Stowe defended herself against
35 such criticism in part by publishing *A Key to Uncle Tom's Cabin* in 1853. This companion to the original novel contains specifics about the actual people whom Stowe had interviewed and upon whom she had based her fictional characters. It also encompasses a more detailed critique of the institution
40 of slavery and the American legal system, which Stowe felt made all whites, even abolitionists, complicit in the subjugation of blacks. The second volume was equally ill-received in the South, with one reviewer claiming that it contained nothing

new; that it was a "distortion of the facts and mutilation of the
45 records, for the sake of ... reduplicating the falsehood of the
representation."

As far-reaching as the book *Uncle Tom's Cabin* was, its sway
over national politics was substantially augmented by stage
adaptations. These "Tom shows" began to be orchestrated even
50 before the end of the original serial publication of the story had
concluded. By some estimates, up to ten times as many people
saw these plays as read the book. While not all productions
were faithful to the original source—some versions were even
pro-slavery—their sheer ubiquity ensured that the book was
55 common cultural currency.

At least one Union general credited Stowe's book with
inspiring his active participation in the abolitionist movement,
and it has become part of the conventional narrative of
American History that the publication of the book was a
60 landmark event in the course of events leading up to the Civil
War. Abraham Lincoln is purported to have said, "So this is the
little lady who started this great war" upon meeting Stowe in
1862, which has solidified her novel's reputation as a catalyst
to the War Between the States. This quote is quite possibly
65 apocryphal; Stowe herself wrote a letter to her husband just
hours after her interview with the president, and made no
mention of the statement. In fact, it makes no appearance in
the historical record until over thirty years after the meeting.

There is no way of verifying the veracity of Lincoln's
70 words, and scholars will undoubtedly continue to debate its
authenticity for years to come. The sentiment it encompasses,
however, is an accurate representation of the perceived import
of the book in the years following the Civil War. A war is
never started in a vacuum, and while we cannot extricate the
75 influence of this one book from its broader cultural and political
milieu, Stowe's intent, to share her belief that "the enslaving
of the African race is a clear violation of the great law which
commands us to love our neighbor as ourselves," remains clear.

Simplify the topic sentence of the first paragraph. Are there
any transitions?

_____

_____

Simplify the topic sentence of the second paragraph. Are
there any transitions?

_____

_____

Simplify the topic sentence of the third paragraph. Are
there any transitions?

_____

_____

Simplify the topic sentence of the fourth paragraph. Are there any transitions?

_____

_____

Simplify the topic sentence of the fifth paragraph. Are there any transitions?

_____

_____

Simplify the topic sentence of the sixth paragraph. Are there any transitions?

_____

_____

Simplify the topic sentence of the seventh paragraph. Are there any transitions?

_____

_____

Remember to follow the following steps for each question:

Step 1: Find the relevant part of the passage.

Step 2: Read (and simplify, if necessary) the relevant part of the passage.

Step 3: POE

1. In the context of the passage, the author's statement that *Uncle Tom's Cabin* "has been eschewed both because of its melodramatic, sentimental style and because of its role in establishing stereotypes of black characters" (lines 4–7) most nearly means that the novel:

   a) is never read today because modern readers find it offensive.
   b) has fallen out of favor with modern readers for a variety of reasons.
   c) is an accurate portrayal of life during the Civil War.
   d) remains a best-seller today because of its historical importance.

2. It can reasonably be inferred by the statement quoted in lines 44–46 that the reviewer meant to express his:

   a) doubt that Stowe had experienced the events in her books first-hand.
   b) admiration for Stowe's accurate portrayal of slaves' lives.
   c) hope that the facts about slavery would be understood.
   d) opinion that *A Key to Uncle Tom's Cabin* was a misleading retelling of the same information in the original novel.

3. In terms of the passage as a whole, one of the main functions of the 5th paragraph (lines 47–55) is to suggest that:

   a) Tom shows were more important than the book they were based on.
   b) stage adaptations of *Uncle Tom's Cabin* helped spread its abolitionist message.
   c) the actors who starred in the stage adaptations of *Uncle Tom's Cabin* became local celebrities.
   d) not all Tom shows faithfully reproduced the book.

4. As it is used in lines 64–65, the phrase *quite possibly apocryphal* most nearly means that Lincoln's statement about Harriet Beecher Stowe:

   a) will never be fully understood.
   b) accurately reflects Stowe's role in advocating for war.
   c) may not be historically accurate, but conveys contemporary opinion.
   d) is untrue because Stowe did not write about it in her letter to her husband.

5. It can reasonably be inferred from the passage that at the time Harriet Beecher Stowe first published *Uncle Tom's Cabin*, federal slavery laws:

   a) had recently been expanded.
   b) were generally unenforced by local law officers.
   c) were less severe than they had been in the late eighteenth century.
   d) inspired controversy in both the North and the South.

Answers and Explanations: Putting It All Together

Simplify the topic sentence of the first paragraph.

> <u>Uncle Tom's Cabin</u> was the best-selling novel of the nineteenth century.

Are there any transitions?

> The transition *although* at the beginning of the sentence tells us that the second part of the sentence is different from the first. The introductory phrase says that *it* (which refers to *Uncle Tom's Cabin*) is not popular today.

Simplify the topic sentence of the second paragraph.

> <u>Stowe penned the novel in response to a law.</u>

Are there any transitions?

> There are no transitions here, which indicates that it's still on the same topic, telling us about *Uncle Tom's Cabin*.

Simplify the topic sentence of the third paragraph.

> <u>The serial was so popular that it was printed in book form.</u>

Are there any transitions?

> Again, no transitions, so we're still talking about more details of *Uncle Tom's Cabin*. If you're not sure what a *serial* is, you can go back to some of the details in the topic sentence of the previous paragraph, which tell you that *Uncle Tom's Cabin* "was originally published as a 40-week serial." So a *serial* has something to do with publishing a book over (in this case) 40 weeks.

Simplify the topic sentence of the fourth paragraph.

> <u>Uncle Tom's Cabin</u> was controversial when it was first published.

Are there any transitions?

> Yes, finally! *Despite* at the beginning of the sentence tells us that the second part of the sentence will tell us something that goes against the idea of popularity. The mention of *popularity* in this beginning phrase shows that the previous paragraph must have been about the popularity of *Uncle Tom's Cabin*, which matches what we already read.

Simplify the topic sentence of the fifth paragraph.

> <u>Uncle Tom's Cabin's</u> sway over politics was augmented by stage adaptations.

Are there any transitions?

> Not really. The first part lets us know that the previous paragraph talked about politics, and the second part tells us that this paragraph will talk about how plays relate to that.

Simplify the topic sentence of the sixth paragraph.

> <u>One guy said *Uncle Tom's Cabin* made him become an abolitionist, and the publication was an event leading up to the Civil War.</u>

Are there any transitions?

> There are not any transitions that tell us that this paragraph is different from what came before, so we're still on the topic of *Uncle Tom's Cabin* and politics. *And* in the middle of the sentence tells us that the two parts are related to each other. The first part of it tells us about how it influenced one guy, and the second part talks about its importance as an event leading up to the Civil War. Remember these ideas are related to each other, so the sentence moves from a small idea (how the book influenced one person) to a big idea (how it was important in history).

Simplify the topic sentence of the seventh paragraph.

> <u>There is no way of verifying Lincoln's words, and people will continue to debate it.</u>

Are there any transitions?

> Just as in the previous paragraph, there are no transitions indicating a change in subject. The beginning of this sentence mentions *Lincoln's words*, which indicates there was probably a quote from Lincoln in the previous paragraph. Again, there's an *and* in the middle of the sentence, telling us that the two parts of the sentence are related: since they can't be verified, people will continue to debate Lincoln's words.

1. **Step 1: Find the relevant part of the passage:** The question directs you to the first paragraph.

   Step 2: Read (and simplify, if necessary) the relevant part of the passage: We already know that *Uncle Tom's Cabin* was popular in the nineteenth century, but is not today. The particular lines this question asks about say that the novel "has been eschewed" in recent years, and then goes on to say why. If you don't know what *eschewed* means, no problem: You know it's not popular today, so it probably has something to do with that.

   Step 3: POE: Choice (a) is too strong. The passage tells us the novel is not popular today, but that's not the same as saying it's never read. Choice (c) is irrelevant to this paragraph. Choice (d) is the opposite of what the passage says. **Choice (b) is correct:** It says *Uncle Tom's Cabin* "has fallen out of favor," which matches the idea in the passage that it's no longer popular.

2. **Step 1: Find the relevant part of the passage:** The question directs you to the end of the fourth paragraph.

   Step 2: Read (and simplify, if necessary) the relevant part of the passage: The topic sentence of the fourth paragraph indicates that the book was controversial when it was first published. The next sentence tells us about criticism of the book, and the following one tells us how Stowe defended herself against criticism by publishing another book. The next sentence, starting with *it also*, gives more detail about this second book, and the final sentence tells about how it, too, was criticized. The quote this question asks about comes from a reviewer who was criticizing the book. If the quote itself is hard to understand, look at the description of what the reviewer said before the semicolon (remember, a semicolon is a same direction transition, so what comes after it is more of the same). That's much more straightforward: "It contained nothing new."

   Step 3: POE: Choice (a) has something to do with the criticism mentioned earlier in the paragraph, about *Uncle Tom's Cabin*, but not with what this quotation refers to. Choice (b) is the opposite—this reviewer did not like Stowe's book. Choice (c) also has the wrong tone—*hope* seems like the reviewer might have liked something, and *facts* is recycled language. **Choice (d) is correct:** The reviewer thought the second book *contained nothing new*, which matches *retelling of the same information*.

3. **Step 1: Find the relevant part of the passage:** The question tells you where to go: the fifth paragraph.

Step 2: Read (and simplify, if necessary) the relevant part of the passage: The topic sentence told us that this paragraph is about how stage versions of *Uncle Tom's Cabin* augmented its political impact. The paragraph then goes on to say that the plays started before the book was even published, and that a whole lot of people saw them. The last sentence may be a little harder to understand, but we get the idea: The message of the book got out partly because lots of people saw plays about it.

Step 3: POE: Choice (a) might sound good on first glance, but the words *more important* don't quite match the passage. The passage says more people *saw* the plays, but it never discusses *importance*. Choice (c) has nothing to do with the passage. Choice (d) is true—it's part of what the last sentence of the paragraph says—but it is not the main idea of the paragraph. **Choice (b) is correct:** Plays helped to spread the message.

4. **Step 1: Find the relevant part of the passage:** The question points you in the right direction, the sixth paragraph.

Step 2: Read (and simplify, if necessary) the relevant part of the passage: This paragraph discusses the influence of *Uncle Tom's Cabin*, big and small. The second sentence gives us the quote from Lincoln that we were expecting to be there, and the next sentence starts with the phrase this question asks about. If you don't know what *apocryphal* means, you can use the context to figure it out. The semicolon is a same direction transition, and after it we're told that Stowe made no mention of this thing Lincoln said, and that there's no record of it until over thirty years later. That all makes it sound like maybe it's made-up, which is probably what *apocryphal* means. If we take a quick look at the beginning of the following sentence, "there is no way of verifying … Lincoln's words," it confirms that idea.

Step 3: POE: What's at issue here is whether Lincoln actually said this thing about Stowe, not whether anyone will ever understand it, so you can eliminate choice (a). Stowe was advocating for abolition of slavery, and while that issue ultimately led to the Civil War, we didn't read anything about her advocating for war, so eliminate choice (b) also. These last two paragraphs discuss *whether* Lincoln's words are historically accurate, but don't say that they're not, so choice (d) is also out. **Choice (c) is correct:** *may not* be true better matches the passage. As far as the second part of the answer choice, there's support for that in the seventh paragraph: "an accurate representation of the perceived import of the book" means pretty much the same thing as "conveys contemporary opinion." Even if you have a hard time understand that part, though, there's good reason to eliminate choices (a), (b), and (d), which leaves choice (c) as the best possibility.

5. **Step 1: Find the relevant part of the passage:** There's no line reference here, but the second paragraph talked about a law that *Uncle Tom's Cabin* was a response to.

    Step 2: Read (and simplify, if necessary) the relevant part of the passage: The second paragraph mentions the Fugitive Slave Law of 1850, and tells us that it was an expansion of an earlier version, from 1793. It also tells us that the law made Stowe mad, which is why she wrote *Uncle Tom's Cabin*.

    Step 3: POE: Choice (b) has nothing to do with the passage. Choice (c) has the change backwards; the law got stricter in 1850. While the law inspired controversy for Stowe at least, the passage doesn't tell us about a more general reaction to it, so eliminate choice (d). **Choice (a) is correct:** The law was expanded in 1850, and Stowe first began to publish *Uncle Tom's Cabin* in 1851.

SUMMARY

- When faced with a difficult reading passage, read the topic sentences first, cutting the fat and simplifying as necessary to understand them.

- Pay close attention to transitions in the topic sentences, and after reading each topic sentence, think about what it tells you about both the previous paragraph and its own paragraph before moving on to the next one.

- When answering questions, first find the relevant part of the passage. If the question doesn't have line references, use what you know about the passage from reading the topic sentences to help you find the right spot.

- Read the relevant portion of the sentence, cutting and simplifying as necessary, but be sure to add important details back in, and use context to help you figure out tough words.

- Finally, use Process of Elimination on the questions. If questions and answers are hard to understand or have tough vocabulary, you can cut and simplify them too.

- Most importantly, remember to focus on what you *can* understand, not what you can't! Most of the time you'll be able to understand enough to answer the question.

Power of the "Word"

Author: Brian Becker

If you're understanding these words right now, you already have the most essential skill on any standardized test: you know how to read. We learn to read when we are very young, so young in fact that we forget what it was like when we *couldn't* read. Now we read all the time. Even if you're not a "reader," if you don't read for pleasure or write creatively, you spend most of your days reading. Whether it's what your teachers write on the board, what your friends send to you in text messages, or the street signs you read on the way to school, you summon your ability to read without even thinking about it.

Even now, stop for a moment and think about how you were able to understand the words in the previous paragraph. You can read and understand English, which is of course the basic requirement, but how do you understand what the words *say*? When we sit back and think about it, reading is a pretty mysterious business. How do we get from basic comprehension to understanding? Are the words magically transformed into meaning in our brains? That couldn't possibly be it.

So in this chapter, let's think about what we're doing when we read.

SENTENCES

In your English classes, you've learned about a large number of literary terms: tone, voice, metaphor, and many, many others. If you have trouble identifying these—especially the first two—you're not alone. Where, after all, are you supposed to look for them? Aren't tone and voice just things that you either get or you don't?

Not exactly. You'll never meet most of the authors that you read, nor will you likely hear them read their work out loud. Because you don't know the person behind the words, then, there must be something in the words themselves that communicates these seemingly incommunicable things.

Reading on standardized tests can be very difficult because you are often punished for making inferences. However, the only bad "inferences" are those that are not rooted in the text. If you can point to particular words and phrases that support a particular inference, then you're no longer working with inferences: You're working with the intended meanings of the texts you are reading.

In this part of the chapter, we'll start with the smallest possible units: words and sentences. You'll be surprised at just how powerful single words can be, but hopefully you will also realize that you've known all along.

I See Where This Is Going: Transitions

Let's say you ask someone out on a date. Which of the following responses would you rather receive?

> *I really like you, and…*

OR

> *I really like you, but…*

I think we'd all much rather hear the first. And why is that? Each sentence only has five words, but the one that's changing makes a big difference. Words like "and" and "but" are what we call *transition words*, and they can change the whole complexion of a sentence.

What would come next? Both sentences start the same way, but they will veer off in very different directions.

> *I really like you, and…*

What might come next?

_____

_____

_____

_____

This word "and" is always linking distinct things. In fact, the word is so common that we've got some different signs for it: & and + are the main ones. The word will always signify continuation or addition. In other words, the words on either side of an "and" will always somehow be in the same category.

In this case, the word "and" is separating two parts of a sentence, so the "and" tells us that those two parts will be linked and continuous somehow. We call words like "and" *same direction* transitions.

Therefore, the second part of the sentence will somehow be a continuation of the first idea: *I really like you.* We'd all like to hear what comes after this! *I really like you, and I'd love to go on a date with you. I really like you, and I've been hoping all semester that you would ask. I really like you, and I'm looking forward to getting to know you better.*

Now, let's say you go on that date. You're unsure of yourself. The movie you wanted to see is sold out. The food at the restaurant is no good. You get to the person's house late. This time, after the date is over, the person turns to you and says,

I really like you, but…

What might come next?

_____

_____

_____

_____

Uh-oh. We probably don't want to hear what's coming next. Notice how that single word *but* allows us to predict what will come next in the sentence. Even though the person still "really likes you," you know something to the contrary is coming next. *I really like you, but I think we should just be friends. I really like you, but I don't think we should go out again. I really like you, but your breath stinks.* All plausible, and all cued by that one little, dreaded word.

Transitions Practice

Let's see how transition words can help us to predict the meanings of a few more sentences. Circle the transition words, and think about whether these are *same direction* or *opposite direction* transitions. You can check your answers at the end of this chapter.

1. While most people believe that "practice makes perfect,"...

   a) the best musicians are those who practice their instruments every day.
   b) I agree strongly with this quote and try to practice it in my daily life.
   c) often the most impressive people in any field are those who were born with some natural ability.
   d) [Cannot be determined from the original sentence]

2. I never go to the grocery store when I'm hungry because ...

   a) being hungry compromises my ability to make wise purchases there.
   b) hunger makes me move more quickly through the store, which I like.
   c) grocery stores are an important feature of most towns.
   d) [Cannot be determined from the original sentence]

3. Although Herman Melville's novels are now widely appreciated,...

   a) Nathaniel Hawthorne was another popular author of Melville's time, though he was a bit older.
   b) some of the novels sold poorly during his lifetime and were not rediscovered until after his death.
   c) Melville's earliest novels, *Typee* and *Omoo*, were "bestsellers" and established Melville's early reputation.
   d) [Cannot be determined from the original sentence]

4. Because so many people watch shows on their computers rather than their televisions these days,...

   a) many networks have started to create original programming that does not appear on television at all.
   b) advertisers are more eager than ever to get their commercials on during television's prime hours.
   c) televisions have become extremely advanced, and some of them have 3-D capability.
   d) [Cannot be determined from the original sentence]

5. Many college graduates go on to great careers even though ...

    a) they work diligently throughout college and get straight As.

    b) they do not graduate from one of the country's "elite" schools.

    c) the number of students going to college each year has risen since the 1970s.

    d) [Cannot be determined from the original sentence]

Now predict what will come before or after each of these sentences. Keep circling transition words and thinking about whether they are *same direction* or *opposite direction* transitions.

6. _____, yet I still haven't heard the band's new album.

7. Scientists have recently discovered what may be a cure for the disease, though _____.

8. The electrician said he would be here by 11 A.M.; however, _____.

9. _____; therefore, I've decided to study a lot in preparation for it.

10. I have no desire to see the new robot movie, nor _____.

Now it's your turn to add the transition words. Choose the word that best fits from each list of answer choices.

11. I'm a little tired of this job, _____ I've decided to look for another one.

    a) but

    b) for

    c) yet

    d) so

12. Goat may be the most-consumed meat in the world, _____ I've never tried it.

    a) thus

    b) but

    c) and

    d) so

13. The weather report today said it was supposed to be sunny, _____ it's raining heavily right now.

    a) therefore
    b) because
    c) yet
    d) and

14. _____ the picnic was rained out, we decided to hold it inside instead.

    a) Although
    b) Despite the fact that
    c) Even though
    d) Because

15. I recently read that it's good to walk a lot; _____, I'm getting off the bus a few stops early and walking the rest of the way.

    a) therefore
    b) however
    c) nevertheless
    d) even so

The Ad-Men: Adjectives and Adverbs

We've seen so far how transition words indicate the relationship between ideas and how those transition words can be used to predict the general flow of sentences. The words also matter within sentences themselves. In this section, we'll look at how single adjectives or adverbs can produce meaning within a sentence.

Let's start with a simple sentence.

> *Michael found the papers.*

This sentence is all content. There's a subject (Michael), a verb (found), and an object (the papers). Believe it or not, we've already got a little more information than this. We know from the word *found* that Michael came across the papers that he had not previously had, and we know from the word *the* that these are some particular papers that have been discussed earlier in the text.

But let's see what happens if we add a single word to this sentence.

> *Suddenly, Michael found the papers.*

Notice how much new information this word adds to the sentence. The sentence has moved beyond the content of its words to *implications*, things that are suggested by the types of words used. On the content level, we know that Michael's discovery of the papers was sudden, but there are a few other implications here as well: We know that Michael had been looking for the papers already, that he was surprised to find them where he did, and that his attitude will change. All that from a single word!

Let's try another.

> *Michael finally found the papers.*

Again, the action remains the same in this sentence: The content has not changed. The implication, however, has changed slightly with the adverb *finally*. With this word, we've got a new sense that Michael has been exasperated looking for the papers and has found them at last. All in that little word *finally*!

We've looked at adverbs. Now let's try adjectives.

> *Michael found the incriminating papers.*

This one is a pretty straightforward use of an adjective—a word that describes a noun. In this case, the word *incriminating* describes the noun, *papers*. While we can't know for sure what Michael's position is (is he a detective? another criminal? an interested party?), we know *which* papers Michael found and why it was significant that those papers were found. They contain something that is incriminating to someone else, and now Michael has them.

Usually, adjectives are pretty straightforward, but let's try one that's a bit more complex.

Michael found the freakin' papers.

Kind of a silly sentence, but what is it that makes it so silly? All the other sentences we've seen so far have contained descriptive words that seem to come from a single source. This one, however, seems to break with that single source with the word *freakin'*. Is this the narrator's word? It literally is, but why would the impersonal narrator have any interest in referring to the papers this way? It's more likely, in fact, that the word *freakin'* is Michael's and that his speech or thought is being represented in this sentence even though he's not directly quoted.

This is a literary device known as *free indirect discourse*. We'll go into more detail about free indirect discourse at the end of the chapter. What we should note here, though, is that this single adjective has clarified a few things about the text that includes this sentence. It shows us that the narrator is writing in a particular way that includes the words and thoughts of the characters without quoting from them. It also shows us that Michael thinks or speaks in a certain way.

Finally, adjectives and adverbs can show up as phrases, especially in older, more elegant writing—the kinds of poems and novels you might have to read for school.

In the writing of an author like Henry James, you're likely to see phrases like this.

Michael found himself of the papers.

Believe it or not, the literal meaning this sentence is the same as that of our original sentence: *Michael found the papers*. In this case, *of the papers* is both a prepositional and adjectival phrase, as in *She is a woman of many talents*, which could be translated as, *She has many talents*.

Why might an author phrase a sentence like this? No one has ever *spoken* this way, so what use could it be to phrase a sentence in such a strange way?

Well, let's look in the middle of the sentence. In the original, the object of the verb *found* is *the papers*. In this case, the object has changed to *himself*. What could this mean? A close reading of these lines might tell us that Michael has found out something about himself in finding the papers, that the papers have given him some new piece of his own identity that he might not have had before.

Sentence structure is a pretty cool thing! As we've seen, words are very potent, and a single word can communicate a good deal more than it seems. In fact, we use these little verbal cues all the time. The trick to becoming a good reader is knowing when you see them and knowing which inferences are supported in the text and which ones are not.

Now, in the following exercises, let's see what we can confidently infer from the statements listed. You can check your answers at the end of this chapter.

16. Ben thought the test was surprisingly difficult.

    a) Ben forgot that he had a test that day.
    b) The test was exactly as hard as Ben expected.
    c) Ben expected the test to be easier.
    d) The whole class thought the test was difficult.

17. Vivian was finally reading *Ulysses* now that she had a break.

    a) *Ulysses* is the last book Vivian will ever read.
    b) Vivian is going to take a break from reading *Ulysses*.
    c) Vivian was just introduced to *Ulysses* on her break.
    d) Vivian has been intending to read *Ulysses* for some time.

18. "Ah, how nice to meet you, the celebrated violinist!"

    a) The violinist is having a party for himself.
    b) The speaker has heard of the violinist from other people or sources.
    c) The speaker and the violinist have met before.
    d) The violinist is disdainful toward the speaker.

19. "No, I'd rather have the salad without feta cheese."

    a) The speaker was initially offered a salad with feta cheese.
    b) The speaker doesn't like any items that have feta cheese on them.
    c) The speaker would prefer an item other than salad.
    d) The speaker has been eating too much salad lately.

20. The largest film industry in the world is actually not that of the United States.

    a) The speaker is shocked to learn that India and Hong Kong have larger film industries.
    b) The speaker is aware of the belief that the U.S. film industry is the largest in the world.
    c) The speaker is condescending to the listener, who doesn't know much about film.
    d) The speaker is covering up the fact that he doesn't know which country has the largest film industry.

A Note on Styles of Discourse

Although all of the examples in the previous section say roughly the same thing, we've seen how single words can give some nuance or additional information to that meaning. Another thing to notice is that different styles of writing draw on different uses of the language. We mentioned that the last sentence is a more literary use of syntax, and the same could be said for *the freakin' papers*, though that one is not so eloquent.

While there is some reasonable variance in how non-fiction prose is written—each author has a style and voice, for example—nearly every type of literary fiction is written in a different way. That's one reason fiction passages on SAT and ACT can be so much tougher to understand.

In a work by a single author, we tend to think of every word as that author's unless we have some reason not to, like quotations or italics. In other words, we think of the author's voice as the sole voice within a passage. However, this is not always the case, and especially since the mid-nineteenth century, literary fiction can be written in many voices at once. Separating those voices from one another is often essential to understanding the meaning of a literary text and an author's own role in it.

In a sentence like this one, there are clearly two voices at work.

> *Stephanie thought, "I can't wait until volleyball season starts again."*

There's one voice inside of quotation marks and one voice outside of them. The voice inside quotation marks is Stephanie's: The quotation marks imply that the words come from Stephanie herself, even if the author of the text is the one who wrote them. The voice outside quotation marks is that of the narrator. We don't always know whether the narrator is the author him- or herself, but in the sentence above, we do know that the narrator's voice is separate from Stephanie's. This kind of sentence, in which the distinctions between narrator and speaker are clear, is called *direct discourse* because the *discourse*, or speech, comes *directly* from the speaker him- or herself.

Sometimes, those voices can appear without quotation marks, but the author can still signal to us that there is more than one voice appearing in the text. Take the following:

> *Stephanie thought to herself that she couldn't wait until volleyball season started again.*

In this sentence, there are no quotations, but it is built much like the first one. Where the first sentence says *Stephanie thought,* this one says *Stephanie thought to herself that.* Then, although it does not appear in quotations, *she couldn't wait until volleyball season started again* is itself a rendering of Stephanie's thought, and as such, it is *indirectly* in Stephanie's voice. This type of speech is called *indirect discourse.* As with direct discourse, the speech is clearly marked, but where direct discourse quotes directly from the speaker, indirect discourse essentially paraphrases the words of the speaker and incorporates them into the narrative voice.

As you know, however, things aren't always quite this easy. Let's try one more.

Stephanie was excited. She couldn't wait *for volleyball to start again!*

Now, there are no quotations in these sentences, so if there's any discourse, it must be indirect. The problem, though, is that there's really no indication from the narrator that Stephanie is the one speaking here—there are no words like *thought, felt,* or *said*. Still, the emphasized word *wait* and the exclamation point at the end of the sentence indicate an emphasis and excitement that is not the narrator's. As we know from the first sentence, it is Stephanie herself who is excited, and this non-quoted, non-specific second sentence must be an indirect rendering of Stephanie's own thoughts.

This complex form of writing is called *free indirect discourse*. It's *indirect discourse,* as in the previous sentence, because it is not quoted. But in this instance, it's *free* because it flows freely in and out of the narrator's speech. Free indirect discourse is an important literary style that was introduced to English writing by Jane Austen in the 1820s. In fact, this style of writing has become so prevalent that we probably don't think of it as having an inventor at all. Moreover, many of the things we think of as literature's assets—psychological probing, layering of voices and perspectives—were only made possible through the literary convention of free indirect discourse. It looks like Jane Austen was doing a lot more than writing beautiful love stories about brainy women and their reluctantly sweet men!

In the following exercise, you are given two sentences. Explain how the word or phrase in the second sentence changes the meaning of the first. You can check your answers at the end of this chapter.

21. Colleen goes to her physics lecture.
    Colleen **seldom** goes to her physics lecture.

    _____

22. Rosita waited for her brother after school.
    Rosita **eagerly** waited for her brother after school.

    _____

23. I ate the rest of the ice cream.
    I **already** ate the rest of the ice cream.

    _____

24. In a rage, Henry threw the chicken salad across the room.

    In a rage, Henry threw **up** the chicken salad across the room.

    _____

25. I've never had good Chinese food.

    I've never **really** had good Chinese food.

    _____

In the following exercise, choose the correct word to fulfill the stated purpose of each sentence.

26. Steven gave up trying to learn the piano: doing so was _____ hard. (*Choose a word that indicates that learning to play the piano is beyond Steven's abilities.*)

    a) very
    b) pretty
    c) too
    d) extremely

27. The two litigants decide to tear _____ the contract and draw up a new one. (*Choose a word that indicates the litigants intend to discard the contract.*)

    a) down
    b) through
    c) into
    d) up

28. It's _____ difficult to find good deals in the months leading up to Christmas (*Choose a word that indicates an extreme difficulty unique to the months described in the sentence compared with other months.*)

    a) really
    b) especially
    c) somewhat
    d) totally

29. James _____ found his way to class. (*Choose a word that indicates that James made his way to class in no particular rush.*)

    a) eventually
    b) hurriedly
    c) once
    d) confusedly

30. This seat is the absolute best _____! (*Choose a word that shows the seat to be the best within a small selection of seats.*)

    a) ever
    b) of all
    c) available
    d) around

So Intense: Synonyms and Changes in Degree

We've seen how single words and phrases can influence the meaning of a particular sentence. With adverbs and adjectives, the nouns and verbs of the sentences stay intact, but they are modified by new words.

We can make some very subtle changes to the words themselves, as well. You've probably used a thesaurus before in hopes that it would spice up your writing in a particular essay. The risk of using a thesaurus, though, is that "synonyms" can be a bit of an overstatement. There are many instances in which synonyms don't mean quite the same thing. Often, writers create subtle shadings in meaning through the strategic use of synonyms.

Let's take a fairly obvious example. The difference between these two sentences is not hard to see.

> *Richard hates his math class.*

> *Richard likes his math class.*

If we change a single word, the whole meaning of the sentence changes very drastically. *Likes* and *hates* are called antonyms (from Greek *anti* (against) and *nym* (name)), and they have opposite meanings from one another.

Things become a little harder to discern, though, when we're working with synonyms. Consider the following two sentences.

> *Richard likes his math class.*

> *Richard loves his math class.*

In this case, the two words are basically synonyms in that they both have a positive meaning, but the difference is one of degree. *Love*, in this case, is an intensification of the word *like*. In other words, if the first sentence tells us that Richard *likes* his math class, the second tells us that he likes his math class a whole lot.

Things get even more difficult with closer synonyms. Consider the following two sentences.

> *Richard loves his math class.*

> *Richard adores his math class.*

In this case, too, *adores* is an intensification of the word *loves*. Though the two sentences mean roughly the same thing, the second sentence indicates that Richard loves his math class a whole lot.

So why do synonyms exist? Is it just because there are a few writers who want to sound fancier than others? Well, sometimes, maybe. It's definitely a demonstration of learning to say *pulchritudinous* rather than *beautiful*, but as we've seen even from the synonyms above, many synonyms aren't quite synonyms. While many synonyms mean roughly the same thing, they usually don't mean *exactly* the same thing, as we've seen with *love* and *adore*, or as you can see between *ugly* and *hideous*, *hate* and *despise*, or *friendly* and *intimate*.

Words without positive and negative connotations can have intensifying synonyms as well. Let's start with a basic sentence.

> *The boy held his mother's hand.*

We can insert a number of synonyms into this sentence that will change the meaning of the sentence. We can make the subject of the sentence either more precise, as in this sentence:

> *The infant held his mother's hand.*

or more general, as in this sentence:

> *The child held his mother's hand.*

The sentences mean roughly the same thing, though the change in subject gives us different information.

Let's see what happens now if we change the verb, *held*, to one of its synonyms.

> *The boy clenched his mother's hand.*

Now the verb no longer seems quite so neutral. *Held* could mean any number of things, but the verb *clenched* suggests that the boy is holding tightly and nervously to his mother's hand. In this case, the synonym *clenched* does the work of the modifying adverbs *tightly* and *nervously*.

How about this sentence?

> *The boy seized his mother's hand.*

In this case, *seized* operates as a synonym for the word *held*, but where *clenched* told us that the boy was nervous or scared, *seized* tells us that the boy is overly aggressive. It looks like these synonyms don't mean quite the same thing after all.

In this exercise, choose the word that intensifies the italicized word. You can check your answers at the end of this chapter.

31. Paul was so hungry that he *ate* all the ice cream.

    a) ingested
    b) devoured
    c) consumed
    d) chewed

32. Linda *enjoyed* the experience of meeting the famous novelist.

    a) partied
    b) liked
    c) did
    d) relished

33. Although tickets were difficult to find, John *wanted* to go the game.

    a) hoped
    b) sought
    c) longed
    d) desired

34. After the game, Patty was so tired that she *lay* down on the ground.

    a) plopped
    b) slept
    c) rested
    d) sat

35. George was tired of watching his friends bicker with each other, so he *left* the house.

    a) went out of
    b) departed
    c) stormed out of
    d) exited

36. Mick was *happy* that he finally understood quadratic equations.

    a) pleased
    b) thrilled
    c) good
    d) content

37. Make sure to take your coat when you go out later—it's *cold* outside.

    a) chilled
    b) lukewarm
    c) freezing
    d) chilly

38. Because he read so many books this summer, Richard has a *big* advantage on the SAT.

    a) literacy
    b) good
    c) tremendous
    d) large

39. The idea of "free trade" was *important* to the economist's theories.

    a) central
    b) notable
    c) significant
    d) financial

40. I usually don't like dogs, but yours is just *cute*.

    a) charming
    b) nice
    c) pretty
    d) adorable

In this exercise, consider the two sentences given in each question. Choose the answer choice that explains how the word change in the second sentence modifies the meaning of the first sentence.

41. I like the pants you picked out, but the shirt is ugly.

    I like the pants you picked out, but the shirt is hideous.

    a) The word *hideous* reduces the severity of the word *ugly*.
    b) The word *hideous* intensifies the word *ugly*.
    c) The word *hideous* changes the meaning of the sentence entirely.
    d) There is no change to the sentence.

42. Around late July, Rory is usually ready to start school again.

    Around late July, Rory is usually eager to start school again.

    a) The word *eager* gives the sentence the opposite meaning from the word *ready*.
    b) The word *ready* shows Rory's preference, whereas the word *eager* is neutral.
    c) The word *eager* shows Rory's preference, whereas the word *ready* is neutral.
    d) There is no change to the sentence.

43. I can't believe I worked so much for such a small paycheck.

    I can't believe I worked so much for such a tiny paycheck.

    a) The word *tiny* intensifies the word *small*.
    b) The word *tiny* reduces the intensity of the word *small*.
    c) The word *tiny* gives the sentence a new, different meaning.
    d) There is no change to the sentence.

44. The bodybuilder's muscles were large.

The bodybuilder's muscles were bulging.

a) The word *bulging* suggests that the muscles are unhealthy.
b) The word *bulging* intensifies the sentence by providing an image.
c) The word *bulging* implies that the bodybuilder should work out more.
d) There is no change to the sentence.

45. The tastes of Coke and Pepsi seem similar to me.

The tastes of Coke and Pepsi seem identical to me.

a) The word *identical* intensifies the word *similar*.
b) The word *identical* provides a more reasonable approach than does the word *similar*.
c) The word *similar* is more specific than the word *identical*.
d) There is no change to the sentence.

46. We were hoping for a good match, but the other school's team beat us.

We were hoping for a good match, but the other school's team destroyed us.

a) The word *beat* works much better with the word *hoping* earlier in the sentence.
b) The word *beat* is not adequately specific to describe the severity of the beating.
c) The word *destroyed* gives a more extreme tone than the word *beat*.
d) There is no change to the sentence.

47. Once he got past security, Jack moved through the embassy.

Once he got past security, Jack crept through the embassy.

a) The word *crept* shows that Jack does not know his way around the embassy.
b) The word *crept* suggests that Jack has something to hide.
c) The word *crept* tells the reader with certainty that Jack is a spy.
d) There is no change to the sentence.

48. Hoping to get to the appointment on time, Gretchen drove through the town.

Hoping to get to the appointment on time, Gretchen raced through the town.

a) The word *raced* describes the manner in which Gretchen *drove*.

b) The word *raced* reduces the intensity of the word *drove*.

c) The word *raced* suggests that Gretchen was competing with another driver.

d) There is no change to the sentence.

49. Because he forgot two years in a row, Bruce said he'd remember his wife's birthday this year.

Because he forgot two years in a row, Bruce swore he'd remember his wife's birthday this year.

a) The word *said* suggests that Bruce has no indication of remembering this year.

b) The word *swore* suggests that Bruce is angry at his wife.

c) The word *said* is neutral, and the word *swore* intensifies it.

d) There is no change to the sentence.

50. In order to understand the philosopher's theories, it's important to read Kant.

In order to understand the philosopher's theories, it's essential to read Kant.

a) The word *essential* suggests that the philosopher's theories cannot be understood without reading Kant.

b) The word *important* suggests that reading Kant is irrelevant to the philosopher's theories.

c) The word *essential* suggests that the philosopher's theories are less important than those of Kant.

d) There is no change to the sentence.

PARAGRAPHS

Now that we have looked at how individual sentences work, we can begin to look at the next unit of writing: the paragraph.

On the one hand, paragraphs are just collections of sentences. If you can pay attention to the language of particular sentences, you can watch those sentences work together to form a bigger thought. A well-written paragraph links its sentences together in a way that makes those links clear and obvious.

On the other hand, paragraphs are much more. In the famous book on writing *The Elements of Style,* written by William Strunk and E.B. White, they offer this advice to writers: "Make the paragraph the unit of composition." In other words, papers, essays, often even stories, are built from paragraphs because paragraphs are fundamentally explorations of ideas.

Think of it this way. If you have to write a ten-page paper, how do you even start? It can be very intimidating if you just start writing and try to get to page 10. Wouldn't it be easier to try to write two five-page papers? Or ten one-page papers? Actually, this is what you're doing all the time, because really, any length of paper is just a collection of paragraphs. The unit of all writing, as Strunk and White say, is the paragraph itself. We might even add that each paragraph is like a little paper itself.

Think about it this way: In every paper or essay, you've got three main tasks. You need to Introduce your idea, Describe it, and then offer a Concluding thought. We can see how this might work in a standard five-paragraph essay.

TASK	ESSAY LEVEL
INTRODUCE	Introductory paragraph
DESCRIBE	Body paragraphs
CONCLUDE	Concluding paragraph

In fact, this works for more than just five-paragraph essays. It can really work for any number of paragraphs. Even most non-fiction books are structured this way.

What you may not realize is that each particular paragraph will follow this same kind of organization. In other words, like the essay itself, each paragraph will have this same structure, even if the terms we use to describe the parts of the paragraph are a little different.

TASK	ESSAY LEVEL	PARAGRAPH LEVEL
INTRODUCE	Introductory paragraph	Topic sentence
DESCRIBE	Body paragraphs	Details in support of the topic sentence
CONCLUDE	Concluding paragraph	Concluding thought that ties back to the main point and transitions to the next

Let's take a simple paragraph as an example.

> *Last Friday, the Philadelphia Flyers beat the Winnipeg Jets. The Flyers opened the scoring only a minute into the game. Although the Jets applied some pressure in the rest of the game, the Flyers were able to fend off the Jets' attacks with some solid defense and outstanding goaltending. The victory seemed tenuous as the Jets applied their full attack at the end of the game, but the Flyers' defense persisted and ensured the team a 2–1 victory. This game was as close as the one a few days later, but both demonstrated that the Flyers are finally turning things around and may be one of the league's best teams by the new year.*

This is the kind of write-up you might see in a newspaper or a sports magazine, and though you can see that this isn't exactly the kind of thing you'd write about in school, the paragraph follows much the same structure as a paragraph on a more academic or complex subject.

Topic sentence: The first sentence introduces the main idea of the paragraph. It tells us that the remainder of the paragraph will discuss the Flyers' win in an earlier game.

Details: The next three sentences describe that particular game. They all support the idea presented in the topic sentence (that the Flyers won), and although there is some new information in these sentences, all the information is given in support of the topic sentence.

Concluding thought: The last sentence shows us both where we are within the paragraph and the essay. From this last sentence, we are prepared for the next paragraph (which will likely describe the game *a few days later*), and we are reminded of the essay's big idea (that *the Flyers are finally turning things around*).

If we were to turn this paragraph into an entire paper, we could just expand each of these three parts. The introductory paragraph could state that the Flyers won and give some of the context for that win. The body paragraphs could describe the reasons that the Flyers won. The concluding paragraph could expand on the ideas given in the last sentence.

Now, this may seem like a writing lesson, so the question is, what does it have to do with reading? First of all, and perhaps obviously, writing and reading are always intertwined. The better you get at writing, the better you'll be able to understand what you're reading and the better you'll be able to see how a piece of writing works. The same goes for reading. The more you read, the more comfortable you'll feel in your own writing.

But beyond that, if we look at how a typical piece of writing is structured, it can help us tremendously with reading comprehension on standardized tests. Just as in the previous section where we used words and phrases to help us understand broader contexts, we can use the structure of a paragraph to help us sift out what's important from what's unimportant and read more efficiently.

A Little Bit of This and a Little Bit of That: Topic Sentences and Transitions

Your English teachers have certainly reminded you of the importance of transitions in your writing. Some teachers might even deduct points or grades from papers that lack these transitions. Sometimes these transitions will be numerical (e.g., *first, second, third*); sometimes they'll be a little more generic (e.g., *next, later, then*); sometimes they'll state contrasts (e.g., *on the other hand, however*); or continuities (e.g., *for example, furthermore*). In many of the things you read on the SAT and ACT, the transitions can be a little more complex or subtle.

So what's the big deal? Why all this emphasis on transitions?

Let's put it as simply as we can: Transitions show the organization of ideas in a paper. Good, clear writing is nearly impossible without good transitions. The things you read on the SAT and ACT (and in many of your high-school and college classes) will nearly always have solid transitions that can help to orient you, the reader, within a piece of writing.

The best transitions are those that *link* one idea to another. Rather than a word that says, "Here's a new idea," the best transitions will say, "Here's a little of what I've been talking about, and here's the next idea that follows from it." If you can spot these transitions, you'll have a clearer sense of what comes before and after them.

Here's a topic sentence from an essay on psychoanalysis.

> By the 1960s, however, Freud's ideas had a firm hold in popular American cultural life.

Let's apply some of what we learned in the previous section on sentences. Pay particular attention to the language and phrasing. Use these words and phrases to predict what the previous paragraph was about and what this new paragraph will be about.

The word *however* tells us right away that this paragraph will be about something in contrast to the previous one. We know, therefore, that the rest of the sentence will be a contrast to something that comes before: *By the 1960s, Freud's ideas had a firm hold in popular American cultural life.*

Then *By the 1960s* tells us that the previous paragraph must've been about an earlier period. Earlier paragraphs must have been about earlier decades. This paragraph will discuss the influence of Freudian ideas in the 1960s, and later paragraphs will likely go on to discuss later decades.

From this sentence, we also learn that *Freud's ideas had a firm hold in popular American cultural life*. Bear in mind that this is a contrast, so the earlier paragraphs must have discussed a time when Freud's ideas did not have this hold, either because people did not know about them or because they actively disagreed with these ideas. The following paragraphs will go on to discuss the hold of these Freudian ideas in decades after the 1960s.

Think about what we've done here. We've built a large part of the essay from a single sentence! We were able to do this because of that sentence's place within a particular paragraph. In a well-constructed non-fiction essay—the type of essay you'll read on the SAT or ACT—the basic outline of the essay, the basic organization of ideas, will appear in the topic sentences.

In the following exercise, use each given sentence to predict what the previous paragraph was about. You can check your answers at the end of this chapter.

1. Many cultural historians suggest that the contemporary attitude toward personifying pets grew out of this shift toward having children at a later age.

   a) The previous paragraph discusses the dominant cultural attitudes toward pets in the United States.
   b) The previous paragraph discusses the shift from adults having children in their early 20s to adults having children in their early 30s.
   c) The previous paragraph discusses the role that cultural historians have played in how pets are treated in the average household.
   d) The previous paragraph discusses the history of domesticated pets in the United States.

2. But once the Washington Nationals drafted Lee Strasberg, the franchise turned around.

   a) The previous paragraph discusses the reasons for the Washington Nationals' continued success in the league.
   b) The previous paragraph discusses Lee Strasberg's life before he started playing baseball.
   c) The previous paragraph discusses the ways that Lee Strasberg helped to improve the team.
   d) The previous paragraph discusses the ill fortunes of the Washington Nationals before the team drafted Lee Strasberg.

3. In the 1890s, furthermore, many other organizations were being founded that rivaled the influence of the American Folklore Society.

   a) The previous paragraph discusses the influence of the American Folklore Society.
   b) The previous paragraph discusses the conditions in the 1890s that produced the American Folklore Society.
   c) The previous paragraph discusses the other organizations that were founded at the same time as the American Folklore Society.
   d) The previous paragraph discusses the history of folklore studies in the United States.

4. All of this changed in the 1960s when Benjamin Quarles republished Frederick Douglass's *Narrative*.

   a) The previous paragraph discusses the major publications that were popular in the 1950s.
   b) The previous paragraph discusses the conditions that would eventually be altered by the publication of Douglass's narrative.
   c) The previous paragraph discusses the important changes that the publication of Frederick Douglass's narrative made possible.
   d) The previous paragraph discusses Frederick Douglass's life and work.

5. It wouldn't be long before the Whig Party got another chance at the White House.

   a) The previous paragraph discusses the basic ideas of which the Whig Party was in favor.
   b) The previous paragraph discusses the connections between the Whig Party and the contemporary Democrats.
   c) The previous paragraph discusses what the Whig Party did when it gained the White House.
   d) The previous paragraph discusses one of the Whig Party's earlier losses.

In this exercise, read each pair of sentences carefully. Choose a topic sentence that links the two of them most effectively.

6. It was just more evidence that I prefer soft mattresses to firm ones.

   _____ Now I can't remember what a soft mattress even feels like.

   a) Throughout my whole life, I've had trouble sleeping.
   b) Last year, I frankly didn't care what kind of mattress I slept on.
   c) But then I bought the firm mattress I still have today.
   d) Firm mattress are actually better for people with bad backs.

7. Certainly, most great musicians will practice many hours a day.

   _____ Many of them could play their instruments before they could read or write.

   a) Some theorize that it takes 10,000 hours to become an "expert" at something.
   b) Still, we can't overlook the natural ability of many of the greatest musicians.
   c) And many musicians like to practice more than they like to play to audiences.
   d) But that doesn't mean that they like it.

8. It was conventional wisdom for many years that disease came from some imbalance within the human being him- or herself.

   _____ For example, waterways, especially those that were heavily used, could be seriously contagious, even for people who weren't bathing in them.

   a) The black plague ripped through many communities in the Middle Ages.
   b) Today, however, we've got penicillin and other drugs to attack those diseases.
   c) People didn't shower as much back then, and restroom facilities were basically non-existent.
   d) In time, though, scientists realized that diseases were made of particles that traveled in unsuspected ways.

9. The house mouse's omnivorous diet means it can survive on just about anything.

   _____ Believe it or not, the average house mouse can fit noiselessly through a hole the size of a U.S. dime.

   a) As it turns out, mice eat a lot more than cheese!
   b) This survival is also aided by the mouse's ability to travel indoors undetected.
   c) Humane traps are becoming much more popular than the old, fatal mousetraps.
   d) Mice are tiny animals, but they can make themselves smaller than you'd think.

10. Often, American tourists are surprised by the difference between the food in China and the "Chinese" food they get in American restaurants.

    _____ Indian-Chinese restaurants, for example, serve Chinese food as it is prepared in India.

    a) India and China share a border just to the northeast of New Delhi.
    b) American tourists have a similar experience when they travel to India.
    c) In fact, Chinese food seems to have adapted to the cuisine in many different countries.
    d) China does not have the problems with obesity that the United States does.

11. As editor of *McClure's,* Willa Cather ultimately learned the tools of her literary trade.

    _____ She ultimately resigned from the position, hoping to devote herself full-time to writing fiction.

    a) *McClure's* was one of many high-cultural publications at the turn of the century.
    b) Cather was well-respected as the editor of *McClure's*, but she had bigger plans.
    c) Willa Cather's best-known novel is *My Antonia*, first published in 1918.
    d) Cather had come a long way from her humble beginnings in Red Cloud, Nebraska.

12. While texting and driving one afternoon, Johnny got into a huge accident and wrecked his car.

    _____ He swore from that day on that he would never text and drive again.

    a) He was uninsured, so all the costs fell to him.
    b) The skies were clear, but the traffic was really bad.
    c) Texting while driving is responsible for many accidents.
    d) With this wake-up call, Johnny had finally learned his lesson.

13. One famous story has a director forcing him, at gunpoint, to learn his lines.

    _____ Who can forget his incredible turn as Stanley Kowalski in *A Streetcar Named Desire*?

    a) Marlon Brando was a star of stage and screen.
    b) Marlon Brando also had problems with Francis Ford Coppola, who directed the great star in *Apocalypse Now.*
    c) For all the problems that he caused, however, Marlon Brando was truly one of the greatest actors of all time.
    d) Under threat of death, Brando eventually learned the lines.

14. All you really need is a ball and court, and even if you're just starting, you can get a great workout.

    _____ It's actually very strategic, and the best players are those who can read the angle of the ball and maintain good tactical positioning.

    a) Racquetball may be easy to learn, but it is very difficult to master.
    b) Racquetball is an indoor racquet sport and was very popular in the 1970s.
    c) Racquetball is fast, and it really stings when the ball hits you.
    d) Racquetball is a great sport for beginners.

15. Audiences didn't always get his jokes, but they loved tuning in to Fred Allen's show on Sundays.

_____ Many of the sponsors would take issue with Allen's commercials, which the sponsors felt were making fun of the products they wanted to sell.

   a) Fred Allen had a famous feud with contemporary radio comedian Jack Benny.
   b) Most radio programs in the 1930s and 1940s had a single sponsor.
   c) Radio commercials are tough to do, especially when it's so easy to switch to another station.
   d) Despite his popular appeal, Allen was always clashing with his sponsors.

In this exercise, read the detail sentences in each question. Choose the topic sentence that those detail sentences most clearly support.

16. John Lennon and Paul McCartney provided the brilliant, endlessly eclectic songwriting. George Harrison contributed some songs of his own and added his quirky touches to Lennon's and McCartney's songs. Ringo Starr provided a driving backbeat that helped to define the band's sound.

   a) Some members of the band were more important than others.
   b) That characteristic "Beatles" sound was the product of all four of the band's members.
   c) Many musicians have written songs and then performed them with other musicians.
   d) The Beatles benefited from the help of a brilliant producer named George Martin.

17. He might have been more politically active as was his contemporary W.E.B. DuBois, but Chesnutt knew that mainstream success would mean more financial rewards. When his novels stopped selling, Chesnutt returned to his work as a lawyer, no longer able to justify writing books that had no audience. Critics have had a terrible time trying to decipher Chesnutt's political message, but in fact, he may not have had one.

   a) Although he has been understood as a great social commentator, Charles Chesnutt was much more interested in making a living than in creating great art.
   b) Charles Chesnutt was one of the first African-American novelists to gain a white audience.
   c) Some of Charles Chesnutt's earliest works were published in the widely read (and still existent) *Atlantic Monthly*.
   d) Like Albion Tourgée before him, Charles Chesnutt started as a lawyer but is best remembered today for his writing.

18. She laid out her nicest dress and ironed it carefully. She went back over the notes she had prepared and reread a few pages of the book. "I'm ready," she said into the mirror, though she still didn't feel completely confident.

    a) Sarah always had a strange habit of talking to herself.
    b) Sarah hadn't done the reading for that day's class.
    c) Sarah usually wore clothes that emphasized comfort over style.
    d) Sarah was nervous to teach her first literature class.

19. For too long, he argues, American economic theory has been relying on the "conventional wisdom" of outdated theories. The ideas of Thomas Malthus and Herbert Spencer were formulated in earlier times when the general economic trends were toward poverty rather than affluence. Even Adam Smith, Galbraith says, can no longer be the guiding light that he inexplicably continues to be.

    a) In the long cycle of booms and busts, American economists have always been ahead of the economic trends they describe.
    b) American economics has a long and storied history, and many theorists from earlier eras continue to influence how we think today.
    c) Kenneth Galbraith suggests that the unprecedented prosperity in the United States requires new economic policies.
    d) Kenneth Galbraith is willing to admit that his own theories draw in large part on those of earlier economists.

20. It was the first of its kind in that it declared British support for the creation of a Jewish homeland. Balfour believed that such a homeland could be created in the British territories in Kenya. The creation of the nation of Israel, that hotly-contested space in the Middle East, is in many ways inconceivable without this document.

    a) Israel has a good deal of historical and spiritual significance for the Jewish religion.
    b) After World War II, many leaders in the free world finally took seriously the idea that the Jewish people should have an officially recognized homeland.
    c) The Balfour Declaration, issued in 1917, was a revolutionary document, the influence of which is difficult to overstate.
    d) The Zionist idea of a Jewish homeland, at least as it is understood by historians, is thought to originate in an 1896 essay by Theodor Herzl.

What Are You Trying to Say? Arguments and Evidence

There are many different types of passages to read. Some essays are meant to inform, others are meant to argue some new point, and still others are meant to make readers laugh, cry, or think in different ways. Typically, the types of writing you will see on standardized tests tend to be one of three types. The first is the story or personal essay. This type of writing doesn't adhere as closely to the traditional paragraph format as many others. In fact, stories and personal essays are usually given as a way to assess your ability to read things like tone and subtlety. As a result, these types of writing are usually best analyzed on the *sentence* level, and the answer to each question will usually hinge on some word or phrase.

The two types of non-fiction prose, expository and persuasive, will adhere much more closely to the traditional paragraph structure because these essays share a basic structure of *Introduce, Describe, Conclude,* whether those three steps are being applied to new information or new arguments. Just as we've seen that each paragraph proves or supports its topic sentence with details, so too does each passage prove or support its main idea or main argument with paragraphs.

In other words, the non-fiction prose on the SAT and ACT will have some *point* that it is trying to get across. This is not to say that fiction or personal writing is "pointless." Think, after all, about your favorite song. What's the "point" of that song? Or your favorite book—does it have some identifiable point? Even if these artistic works do have some point, it's not a point that everyone would agree on, nor is it the kind of thing you could identify in the few minutes you have on a standardized test.

In writing that *does* have a point, then, where do you find that point? Some English teachers will ask you to underline the thesis statements in your papers, but this doesn't usually happen in non-academic writing, and it *definitely* won't happen on the SAT or ACT. Of all the words and sentences in a piece of writing, how do you know which ones matter the most?

First and foremost, it helps to think about *why* a particular piece of writing exists. Who might care about this particular piece of writing? What does a reader gain from reading it?

Think about it this way. If you wanted to read something about William Shakespeare, you'd actually have to make a lot of choices before you started reading at all. If you wanted a basic outline of Shakespeare's life, you might go to an encyclopedia. If you wanted a review of a new performance of one of Shakespeare's plays, you'd probably go to a newspaper or entertainment magazine. If you wanted a more thorough description of Shakespeare's life and times, you'd probably go to a biography. If you wanted a summary of one of Shakespeare's plays, you'd probably go to Sparknotes or Cliff's Notes. If you wanted a broad interpretation of Shakespeare's plays, you might go to a book of literary criticism.

Each of these pieces of writing is in some way about the same topic, Shakespeare, but each one gives the reader something different. When you pick out the books or articles yourself, you know what you're getting. When your teacher assigns them, you know a little less, but even so, you know more than you think. For example, you'll read a book differently for your science class than you will for your literature class. A science textbook contains facts that you may need to memorize; a novel or short story requires a different set of interpretive skills. You might read a novel in one way if you're reading it for pleasure, another way if you're reading it for an exam, and still another if you're reading it to write an essay.

On a standardized test, you're given even less information. You will have to answer some questions about the reading, but you don't know much more than that. As a result, any preliminary reading that you do should be geared toward answering the question, "What's the point?"

Look at these two sentences, and try to think about which one would be more likely to be part of the "point" of an essay.

> *Zora Neale Hurston was born in 1891.*

> *Zora Neale Hurston was actually born in 1891.*

Both sentences contain similar information. It is a fact that the author Zora Neale Hurston was born in 1891, and that fact alone is not likely to be the "point" of any particular essay.

Notice, though, what the word "actually" does in the second sentence. As we saw in the first part of this chapter, single words can have a huge influence on the meanings of particular sentences. In this case, the word "actually" implies that the year of Hurston's birth is the subject of some doubt or misconception. From this single word, we know that we are getting close to the main point of the article. The person reading this essay is presumed not to know the actual year of Hurston's birth, and one of the points of this essay will likely be to correct that misconception and to make some larger point out of it.

We might call words like "actually" the *language of argument*. If we can find this language of argument within a particular passage, we can get closer to the passage's central argument or main point. The "point" of many pieces of writing is to inform the reader of something he or she did not know. Because of this basic structure, the language of argument usually implies some kind of disagreement or something to be corrected.

Which of these sentences contains the language of argument?

> *We're going to the donut shop tomorrow.*

> *We're going to the donut shop too often.*

The second sentence contains the language of argument. Notice how the words *too often* suggest what will come next, probably something like, *We should stop going so much.* The first sentence is merely descriptive. Any number of things could follow from it, and it doesn't contain any of the larger implications necessary for a "point."

When you choose the things that you read, it's up to you to determine whether they have value or not, whether the "point" of them is relevant to you. When you are assigned reading, whether in class or on a standardized test, you lose this choice. It has already been determined, either by your teacher or by the writers of the test, that these readings have a point, and the earlier you are able to find that point, the more successful you will be when your comprehension of that reading is tested.

In this exercise, determine whether each sentence contains the language of argument (LOA) and identify that language. You can check your answers at the end of this chapter.

21. It is commonly thought that chicken is one of the healthier meats.

    a) Contains LOA in the words *commonly thought*
    b) Contains LOA in the word *chicken*
    c) Contains LOA in the words *healthier meats*
    d) Does not contain LOA

22. My mom will probably make pecan pie this Thanksgiving.

    a) Contains LOA in the words *my mom*
    b) Contains LOA in the word *probably*
    c) Contains LOA in the words *this Thanksgiving*
    d) Does not contain LOA

23. We all know that General Custer died in the Battle of Little Big Horn.

    a) Contains LOA in the words *we all know*
    b) Contains LOA in the word *died*
    c) Contains LOA in the words *the Battle*
    d) Does not contain LOA

24. And here you thought we wouldn't be here on time!

    a) Contains LOA in the words *and here*
    b) Contains LOA in the words *you thought*
    c) Contains LOA in the word *here*
    d) Does not contain LOA

25. The two ice cream flavors are really not that different.

    a) Contains LOA in the word *two*
    b) Contains LOA in the words *ice cream flavors*
    c) Contains LOA in the words *really not that*
    d) Does not contain LOA

26. Mark Twain wrote *The Adventures of Huckleberry Finn* over the span of a few years.

    a) Contains LOA in the word *wrote*
    b) Contains LOA in the words *over the span*
    c) Contains LOA in the words *a few years*
    d) Does not contain LOA

27. Many people believe that the best baseball teams are those that hit the most home runs.

    a) Contains LOA in the words *many people*
    b) Contains LOA in the words *those*
    c) Contains LOA in the words *the most*
    d) Does not contain LOA

28. It may be time to bring out the polka dots again.

    a) Contains LOA in the words *may be*
    b) Contains LOA in the words *bring out*
    c) Contains LOA in the word *again*
    d) Does not contain LOA

29. The first stop on my cross-country road trip was Chicago, IL.

    a) Contains LOA in the words *first stop*
    b) Contains LOA in the word *cross-country*
    c) Contains LOA in the word *was*
    d) Does not contain LOA

30. As a boy, I thought I would never like American cheese.

    a) Contains LOA in the words *As a boy*
    b) Contains LOA in the words *I thought*
    c) Contains LOA in the words *American cheese*
    d) Does not contain LOA

In the following exercise, read each sentence carefully. Look for the language of argument, and choose the answer that is most clearly implied by this language of argument.

31. Contrary to popular belief, the iPhone is really not that much better than other smartphones.

    a) Most people believe that non-iPhone smartphones are ineffective.
    b) The iPhone is the best of all smartphones except in a few key areas.
    c) Many people think the iPhone is better than other smartphones.
    d) Does not contain the language of argument

32. In the band's early days, Pink Floyd was actually led by a singer named Syd Barrett.

   a) Pink Floyd used to be known by a different name.
   b) Some believe the band's best-known singer was always the singer of the band.
   c) Syd Barrett stayed in Pink Floyd, though he was not the band's lead singer.
   d) Does not contain the language of argument

33. Do you really believe the tooth fairy took your tooth last night?

   a) The speaker does not believe the tooth fairy took your tooth.
   b) The speaker believes the tooth fairy took your tooth late last week.
   c) The speaker believes you are stupid for thinking this way.
   d) Does not contain the language of argument

34. The Detroit Lions are the only team in modern NFL history to go through a whole season without winning a game.

   a) The writer believes that the Detroit Lions are the worst team in the NFL.
   b) The writer is disgusted by this terrible performance by the Lions.
   c) There are other teams who have done the same in other sports.
   d) Does not contain the language of argument

35. Against the conventional wisdom, some scientists are starting to argue again for the health benefits of milk.

   a) The scientists who put forth this argument do not believe in conventional wisdom.
   b) The conventional wisdom about milk's health benefits is correct.
   c) It is widely believed that milk is not a healthy thing to consume.
   d) Does not contain the language of argument

36. David somehow managed to flunk his Spanish class.

   a) David has not flunked a class before.
   b) David was expected to pass his Spanish class.
   c) David is very good at speaking Spanish.
   d) Does not contain the language of argument

37. No one thought it possible that an NHL team could win three Stanley Cups in a row.

    a) The average hockey fan does not understand the sport.
    b) An NHL team could still win three Stanley Cups in a row.
    c) An NHL team did win three Stanley Cups in a row.
    d) Does not contain the language of argument

38. The food at this Thai restaurant is too spicy.

    a) Most Thai restaurants use too much hot pepper.
    b) The speaker would prefer to eat Thai food elsewhere.
    c) The speaker does not like Thai food.
    d) Does not contain the language of argument

39. Apples are a good source of fiber, and two-thirds of that fiber is in the apple's skin.

    a) Many scientists believe apples do not contain any fiber.
    b) It is commonly believed that all an apple's fiber is in its core.
    c) Apples are the best source of fiber of any fruit or vegetable.
    d) Does not contain the language of argument

40. Those in education are overly committed to the idea that math and science are the subjects with the most relevance to the contemporary workplace.

    a) Students who are good at math and science have the best chance at successful careers.
    b) The education system in the United States is broken.
    c) Subjects other than math and science have workplace relevance.
    d) Does not contain the language of argument

In this exercise, read each paragraph. Identify the sentence that contains the paragraph's main point.

41. (1) Baz Luhrmann's adaptation of *The Great Gatsby* received both praise and criticism. (2) Those who liked the novel best tended to criticize Luhrmann's adaptation. (3) Those who had not read the novel tended to like the film. (4) In my view, however, there's something in Luhrmann's adaptation for everyone.

    a) 1
    b) 2
    c) 3
    d) 4

42. (1) T-Bone steaks, hamburgers, filet mignon. (2) Red meat has long been a staple of the American diet. (3) Farmers in many regions of the country have produced some of the best beef in the world. (4) Beef has become as American as apple pie.

   a) 1
   b) 2
   c) 3
   d) 4

43. (1) The women in Ernest Hemingway's novels regularly find themselves in compromising situations. (2) They are often reduced to objects of men's desires or limited in the way they can act. (3) Critics have taken issue with Hemingway's portrayal of women, arguing that Hemingway himself is sexist. (4) However, a closer look reveals that Hemingway is more sensitive to the plight of women than we might believe.

   a) 1
   b) 2
   c) 3
   d) 4

44. (1) I grew up thinking that I would never be any good at tennis. (2) My serves always went out. (3) I couldn't hit a backhand to save my life. (4) And my arms got so tired early in all of my matches.

   a) 1
   b) 2
   c) 3
   d) 4

45. (1) Slavery was well-established in the United States in the early 1800s. (2) There were slaveowners in the Northern states as well as the Southern ones. (3) All of this started to change in the 1820s. (4) This decade would later be known as the early period of the "American Renaissance."

   a) 1
   b) 2
   c) 3
   d) 4

PASSAGES

Now that we have looked at the smaller units of reading passages, let's try to apply what we have learned to longer passages. These passages are more difficult than anything you're likely to see on the SAT or the ACT, but you will find that applying what you've learned so far can make understanding these passages much easier. You can check your answers at the end of this chapter.

The first passage comes from a lecture by William James entitled "What Pragmatism Means."

[1]

(1) Some years ago, being with a camping party in the mountains, I returned from a solitary ramble to find every one engaged in a ferocious metaphysical dispute. (2) The corpus of the dispute was a squirrel—a live squirrel supposed to be clinging to one side of a tree-trunk; while over against the tree's opposite side a human being was imagined to stand. (3) This human witness tries to get sight of the squirrel by moving rapidly round the tree, but no matter how fast he goes, the squirrel moves as fast in the opposite direction, and always keeps the tree between himself and the man, so that never a glimpse of him is caught. (4) The resultant metaphysical problem now is this: Does the man go round the squirrel or not? (5) He goes round the tree, sure enough, and the squirrel is on the tree; but does he go round the squirrel? (6) In the unlimited leisure of the wilderness, discussion had been worn threadbare. (7) Every one had taken sides, and was obstinate; and the numbers on both sides were even. (8) Each side, when I appeared therefore appealed to me to make it a majority. (9) Mindful of the scholastic adage that whenever you meet a contradiction you must make a distinction, I immediately sought and found one, as follows: "Which party is right," I said, "depends on what you practically mean by 'going round' the squirrel. (10) If you mean passing from the north of him to the east, then to the south, then to the west, and then to the north of him again, obviously the man does go round him, for he occupies these successive positions. (11) But if on the contrary you mean being first in front of him, then on the right of him, then behind him, then on his left, and finally in front again, it is quite as obvious that the man fails to go round him, for by the compensating movements the squirrel makes, he keeps his belly turned towards the man all the time, and his back turned away. (12) Make the distinction, and there is no occasion for any farther dispute. (13) You are both right and both wrong according as you conceive the verb 'to go round' in one practical fashion or the other."

[2]

(1) Although one or two of the hotter disputants called my speech a shuffling evasion, saying they wanted no quibbling or scholastic hair-splitting, but meant just plain honest English 'round,' the majority seemed to think that the distinction had assuaged the dispute.

(1) I tell this trivial anecdote because it is a peculiarly simple example of what I wish now to speak of as the pragmatic method. (2) The pragmatic method is primarily a method of settling metaphysical disputes that otherwise might be interminable. (3) Is the world one or many?—fated or free?—material or spiritual?—here are notions either of which may or may not hold good of the world; and disputes over such notions are unending. (4) The pragmatic method in such cases is to try to interpret each notion by tracing its respective practical consequences. (5) What difference would it practically make to any one if this notion rather than that notion were true? (6) If no practical difference whatever can be traced, then the alternatives mean practically the same thing, and all dispute is idle. (7) Whenever a dispute is serious, we ought to be able to show some practical difference that must follow from one side or the other's being right.

1   In the first sentence, the author uses the word *ferocious*. If he had not used this word, the sentence would read as follows: *I returned from a solitary ramble to find everyone engaged in a metaphysical debate.* How does the word *ferocious* alter this statement?

   a)   The word *ferocious* indicates that the debate concerned the subject of violence in society.
   b)   The word *ferocious* helps to underline how heated the debate had become.
   c)   The word *ferocious* suggests that those participating in the debate were acting violently.
   d)   The word does not make a difference.

2.   What is the subject of this *ferocious metaphysical debate*?

   a)   Violence in society
   b)   The existence of God
   c)   A squirrel
   d)   The wilderness

3.   Consider your answers to questions 1 and 2. What kind of tone does the author create, and how does the first sentence create it?

   a)   Confused, because the author does not understand metaphysical debates.
   b)   Dismissive, because the author prefers his solitary walk to the ferocious debate.
   c)   Cruel, because no one likes to be in the middle of a ferocious debate in the wilderness.
   d)   Humorous, because there is something silly about having a ferocious debate about squirrels.

4. Which side does the author choose in the metaphysical debate?

   a) He agrees with those who say the man goes around the squirrel.
   b) He agrees with those who say the man does not go around the squirrel.
   c) He says both sides are right and wrong depending on some other definitions.
   d) He does not comment and returns to his solitary walk in the woods.

5. What is the "point" sentence of the first paragraph?

   a) 2
   b) 4
   c) 7
   d) There is no point sentence in this paragraph.

6. The author admits that his anecdote is *trivial*, so why does he include it?

   a) He wants to show that he is much smarter than most other people.
   b) He wants to indicate that he ultimately sided with one group over the other.
   c) He wishes to show that people can be wrong about the simplest things.
   d) He wants to give simple instance of the more complex subject he wishes to discuss.

7. Which of the following is NOT an example of one of the *metaphysical disputes that otherwise might be interminable*?

   a) Is the world fated or free?
   b) What does pragmatism mean?
   c) Does the man go around the squirrel?
   d) Is the world one or many?

8. What could make a metaphysical question *serious* rather than *idle*?

   a) A practical difference between the sides of the argument
   b) Ferocity in debating the subject
   c) Concern with life's greatest mysteries
   d) Alternatives that mean practically the same thing

9. What is the pragmatic method?

   a) A philosophy that treats all questions as serious rather than idle
   b) A style of analysis that focuses on practical consequences
   c) Something that can be practiced in the *unlimited leisure of the wilderness*
   d) A style of debate that promotes *ferocious* arguing

10. Which of the following sentences best summarizes the "point" of the passage?

   a) Paragraph 1, Sentence 3
   b) Paragraph 1, Sentence 11
   c) Paragraph 2, Sentence 1
   d) Paragraph 3, Sentence 4

This passage comes from *Women and Economics* by Charlotte Perkins Gilman

[1]

(1) Since we have learned to study the development of human life as we study the evolution of species throughout the animal kingdom, some peculiar phenomena which have puzzled the philosopher and moralist for so long, begin to show themselves in a new light. (2) We begin to see that, so far from being inscrutable problems, requiring another life to explain, these sorrows and perplexities of our lives are but the natural results of natural causes, and that, as soon as we ascertain the causes, we can do much to remove them.

[2]

(1) In spite of the power of the individual will to struggle against conditions, to resist them for a while, and sometimes to overcome them, it remains true that the human creature is affected by his environment, as is every other living thing. (2) The power of the individual will to resist natural law is well proven by the life and death of the ascetic. (3) In any one of those suicidal martyrs may be seen the will, misdirected by the ill-informed intelligence, forcing the body to defy every natural impulse,—even to the door of death, and through it.

[3]

(1) But, while these exceptions show what the human will can do, the general course of life shows the inexorable effect of conditions upon humanity. (2) Of these conditions we share with other living things the environment of the material universe. (3) We are affected by climate and locality, by physical, chemical, electrical forces, as are all animals and plants. (4) With the animals, we farther share the effect of our own activity, the reactionary force of exercise. (5) What we do, as well as what is done to us, makes us what we are. (6) But, beyond these forces, we come under the effect of a third set of conditions peculiar to our human status; namely, social conditions. (7) In the organic interchanges which constitute

social life, we are affected by each other to a degree beyond what is found even among the most gregarious of animals. (8) This third factor, the social environment, is of enormous force as a modifier of human life. (9) Throughout all these environing conditions, those which affect us through our economic necessities are most marked in their influence.

[4]

(1) Without touching yet upon the influence of the social factors, treating the human being merely as an individual animal, we see that he is modified most by his economic conditions, as is every other animal. (2) Differ as they may in color and size, in strength and speed, in minor adaptation to minor conditions, all animals that live on grass have distinctive traits in common, and all animals that eat flesh have distinctive traits in common—so distinctive and so common that it is by teeth, by nutritive apparatus in general, that they are classified, rather than by means of defence or locomotion. (3) The food supply of the animal is the largest passive factor in his development; the processes by which he obtains his food supply, the largest active factor in his development. (4) It is these activities, the incessant repetition of the exertions by which he is fed, which most modify his structure and develop his functions. (5) The sheep, the cow, the deer, differ in their adaptation to the weather, their locomotive ability, their means of defence; but they agree in main characteristics, because of their common method of nutrition.

11. What has enabled the author to see some human problems *in a new light*?

    a)   A new finding that shows the ways humans and animals are different
    b)   A new group of philosophers with new ideas
    c)   A new way of describing lives of other species
    d)   A refusal to be puzzled by the irrelevant problems of older philosophies

12. What has the study of the *evolution of species* shown the author?

    a)   Human life is filled with sorrow and confusion.
    b)   Human life is shaped by the environment in which humans live.
    c)   Evolutionary ideas apply to the animal kingdom but not to humans.
    d)   Human life can only be understood by natural scientists.

13. Which of the following quotations best shows the value of understanding environmental causes in influencing human life?

    a) "inscrutable problems, requiring another life to explain"
    b) "these sorrows and perplexities of our lives"
    c) "as soon as we ascertain the causes"
    d) "we can do much to remove them"

14. Identify the language of argument in the first sentence of the second paragraph.

    a) "in spite of" and "remains true"
    b) "struggle against" and "for a while"
    c) "affected" and "living thing"
    d) "individual will" and "environment"

15. What is the "point" sentence in the second paragraph?

    a) 1
    b) 2
    c) 3
    d) There is no point sentence in the second paragraph.

16. The second sentence of the third paragraph reads, "Of these conditions we share with other living things the environment of the material universe." How does the mention of *other living things* relate to the point made in the first paragraph about the *evolution of species*?

    a) The study of the evolution of other living things reveals all the conditions to which human beings are not subject.
    b) The study of the evolution of other living things was made possible by philosophers' insistence on seeing them in a new light.
    c) The study of the evolution of other living things presents a series of inscrutable problems.
    d) The study of the evolution of other living things has revealed new things about human beings.

17. Use the topic sentences of the second, third, and fourth paragraphs to identify how these paragraphs relate to one another.

    a) Paragraph 2 discusses religious martyrs; Paragraph 3 discusses the weather; and Paragraph 4 discusses the eating habits of animals.
    b) Paragraph 2 discusses the importance of environmental conditions; Paragraph 3 lists some of those conditions; and Paragraph 4 identifies the most important condition.
    c) Paragraph 2 discusses human beings' ability to resist the natural world; Paragraph 3 lists some exceptions to the general rule; and Paragraph 4 shifts the focus to economics.
    d) Paragraph 2 discusses individual human beings; Paragraph 3 discusses animals; and Paragraph 4 discusses both human beings and animals.

18. According to the author, what is the single most important condition that influences human behavior?

    a) Climate
    b) Diet
    c) Chemistry
    d) Economy

19. Why does the author end the fourth paragraph by discussing the role of food?

    a) She believes that what one does to obtain food influences many other behaviors.
    b) She believes that the types of food that one eats influence one's economic output.
    c) She believes that cows, sheep, and human beings are identical because they all eat natural foods.
    d) She believes that humans that eat cows and sheep are economically superior to those animals.

20. Which of the following sentences best summarizes the "point" of the passage?

    a) Paragraph 1, Sentence 1
    b) Paragraph 2, Sentence 3
    c) Paragraph 3, Sentence 4
    d) Paragraph 4, Sentence 1

This comes from Franklin Roosevelt's 1933 "Fireside Chat" on the banking crisis that caused the Great Depression.

[1]

(1) We had a bad banking situation. (2) Some of our bankers had shown themselves either incompetent or dishonest in their handling of the people's funds. (3) They had used the money entrusted to them in speculations and unwise loans. (4) This was of course not true in the vast majority of our banks but it was true in enough of them to shock the people for a time into a sense of insecurity and to put them into a frame of mind where they did not differentiate, but seemed to assume that the acts of a comparative few had tainted them all. (5) It was the Government's job to straighten out this situation and do it as quickly as possible—and the job is being performed.

[2]

(1) I do not promise you that every bank will be reopened or that individual losses will not be suffered, but there will be no losses that possibly could be avoided; and there would have been more and greater losses had we continued to drift. (2) I can even promise you salvation for some at least of the sorely pressed banks. (3) We shall be engaged not merely in reopening sound banks but in the creation of sound banks through reorganization. (4) It has been wonderful to me to catch the note of confidence from all over the country. (5) I can never be

sufficiently grateful to the people for the loyal support they have given me in their acceptance of the judgment that has dictated our course, even though all of our processes may not have seemed clear to them.

[3]

(1) After all there is an element in the readjustment of our financial system more important than currency, more important than gold, and that is the confidence of the people. (2) Confidence and courage are the essentials of success in carrying out our plan. (3) You people must have faith; you must not be stampeded by rumors or guesses. (4) Let us unite in banishing fear. (5) We have provided the machinery to restore our financial system; it is up to you to support and make it work.

[4]

(1) It is your problem no less than it is mine. (2) Together we cannot fail.

21. How would the second sentence of the first paragraph be changed if the words "Some of" were removed?

   a) It would suggest that all bankers contributed to the bad banking situation.
   b) It would name the specific bankers who were responsible for the bad banking situation.
   c) It would indicate that the bad banking situation does not apply to everyone.
   d) It would more clearly describe the reasons for the bad banking situation.

22. In the third sentence of the first paragraph, to whom does the word "They" refer?

   a) All bankers in the American banking system
   b) The bankers who acted in incompetent or dishonest ways
   c) The American people who entrusted their money to banks
   d) The government officials who allowed unethical bankers to thrive

23. Consider your answers to the first two questions. What is the speaker trying to do in separating one group out from another?

   a) To show the extent of the *bad banking situation*
   b) To demonstrate what happened with the *vast majority* of bankers
   c) To *shock the people* into recognizing the extent of the banking crisis
   d) To *differentiate* the few bad bankers from the many good ones

24. What is the "point" sentence of the first paragraph?

    a) 1
    b) 2
    c) 3
    d) 4

25. The speaker begins the second paragraph with the words "I do not promise you...." Is this the language of argument? If yes, what does it imply?

    a) No, this is not the language of argument.
    b) Yes, it suggests that there is something that the speaker does promise.
    c) Yes, it suggests that people have been too demanding of the speaker.
    d) Yes, it suggests that the speaker has done all that he can.

26. In the last sentence of the second paragraph, how would the meaning of the sentence change if the word "sufficiently" were removed?

    a) The sentence would then indicate that the speaker will continue without the public's support.
    b) The sentence would then state that the speaker did not appreciate the public's support.
    c) The sentence would then show the speaker's true appreciation for the public's support.
    d) The sentence would be unchanged.

27. In the last sentence of the second paragraph, the speaker is especially grateful for the "acceptance" that the American public has given his plan. What is notable about this acceptance?

    a) The president appreciates this acceptance, but he is ungrateful for it.
    b) Many people accept the president's plan even though it aids unethical bankers.
    c) The majority of people accept the plan, but a vocal minority rejects it.
    d) The public gives its acceptance, but it may not understand what it is accepting.

28. Why does the speaker use the word "stampeded" rather than a more neutral word like "influenced"?

    a) "Stampeded" suggests a violence and unreasonableness to the rumors and guesses of people who disagree with his plan.
    b) "Stampeded" suggests the extent of the damage that the bad banking system has done to the country.
    c) "Stampeded" suggests the type of action the public can be expected to take against unethical bankers.
    d) The more neutral word would make no difference.

29. Consider the language you have analyzed in the previous questions. How is the speaker portraying himself?

   a) As a man who is level-headed, able to separate the good from the bad, and who therefore deserves the public's trust
   b) As a man who is fearful of the power of the banks, unsure how to proceed, and overly concerned with public approval
   c) As a man who has been stampeded by public disapproval, rejected by bankers, and committed to an idea that may not work
   d) As a man who refuses to make promises, separates himself from the general public, and sides with bankers over ordinary citizens

30. Which of the following sentences best summarizes the "point" of the passage?

   a) Paragraph 1, Sentence 1
   b) Paragraph 2, Sentence 2
   c) Paragraph 3, Sentence 5
   d) Paragraph 4, Sentence 1

This passage comes from a speech by Frederick Douglass entitled "The Hypocrisy of American Slavery."

[1]

(1) Fellow citizens, pardon me, and allow me to ask, why am I called upon to speak here today? (2) What have I or those I represent to do with your national independence? (3) Are the great principles of political freedom and of natural justice, embodied in that Declaration of Independence, extended to us? (4) And am I, therefore, called upon to bring our humble offering to the national altar, and to confess the benefits, and express devout gratitude for the blessings resulting from your independence to us?

[2]

(1) Would to God, both for your sakes and ours, that an affirmative answer could be truthfully returned to these questions. (2) Then would my task be light, and my burden easy and delightful. (3) For who is there so cold that a nation's sympathy could not warm him? (4) Who so obdurate and dead to the claims of gratitude that would not thankfully acknowledge such priceless benefits? (5) Who so stolid and selfish that would not give his voice to swell the hallelujahs of a nation's jubilee, when the chains of servitude had been torn from his limbs? (6) I am not that man. (7) In a case like that, the dumb might eloquently speak, and the "lame man leap as an hart."

[3]

(1) But such is not the state of the case. (2) I say it with a sad sense of disparity between us. (3) I am not included within the pale of this glorious anniversary! (4) Your high independence only reveals the immeasurable distance between us. (5) The blessings in which you this day rejoice are not enjoyed in common. (6) The rich inheritance of justice, liberty, prosperity, and independence bequeathed by your fathers is shared by you, not by me. (7) The sunlight that brought life and healing to you has brought stripes and death to me. (8) This Fourth of July is yours, not mine. (9) You may rejoice, I must mourn. (10) To drag a man in fetters into the grand illuminated temple of liberty, and call upon him to join you in joyous anthems, were inhuman mockery and sacrilegious irony. (11) Do you mean, citizens, to mock me, by asking me to speak today? (12) If so, there is a parallel to your conduct. (13) And let me warn you, that it is dangerous to copy the example of a nation (Babylon) whose crimes, towering up to heaven, were thrown down by the breath of the Almighty, burying that nation in irrecoverable ruin.

[4]

(1) Fellow citizens, above your national, tumultuous joy, I hear the mournful wail of millions, whose chains, heavy and grievous yesterday, are today rendered more intolerable by the jubilant shouts that reach them. (2) If I do forget, if I do not remember those bleeding children of sorrow this day, "may my right hand forget her cunning, and may my tongue cleave to the roof of my mouth!"

[5]

(1) To forget them, to pass lightly over their wrongs and to chime in with the popular theme would be treason most scandalous and shocking, and would make me a reproach before God and the world.

[6]

(1) My subject, then, fellow citizens, is "American Slavery." (2) I shall see this day and its popular characteristics from the slave's point of view. (3) Standing here, identified with the American bondman, making his wrongs mine, I do not hesitate to declare, with all my soul, that the character and conduct of this nation never looked blacker to me than on this Fourth of July.

31. Look at the questions in the first two paragraphs. Why does the speaker ask them?

   a) He is hoping someone from the audience will respond with the correct answer.
   b) He is unsure what he is supposed to be talking about and is looking for help from the crowd.
   c) He is trying to adapt his speech to the interests of those in the crowd.
   d) He is setting up a series of answers that will lead to his main point.

32. What is the answer to the questions in the first paragraph?

   a) Yes
   b) No
   c) Maybe
   d) The speaker doesn't give an answer.

33. What would make the speaker's task *light* and his burden *easy and delightful*?

   a) If the answer to all the first paragraph's questions were "Yes"
   b) If the answer to all the first paragraph's questions were "No"
   c) If the audience were more receptive to the speaker's ideas
   d) If the audience would provide thorough answers to the speaker's questions

34. Look at the use of pronouns (*us, you, me*) in the third paragraph. How is each one used?

   a) *Us* is used to describe a common trait; *you* is the audience who asks questions; and *me* is the speaker who seeks to answer those questions.
   b) *Us* is used to describe a difference; *you* is the audience who cannot celebrate the 4th of July; and *me* is the speaker who celebrates it proudly.
   c) *Us* is used to describe a common trait; *you* is the audience celebrating the 4th of July; and *me* is the speaker who is answering questions.
   d) *Us* is used to describe a difference; *you* is the audience celebrating the 4th of July; and *me* is the speaker who cannot share in the celebration.

35. Which of the following is one of the "point" sentences of the third paragraph?

   a) 1
   b) 8
   c) 11
   d) 13

36. Who are the *millions* referred to fourth paragraph? Pay close attention to the language of this paragraph and look at the topic sentences of later paragraphs.

   a) Babylonians
   b) The audience
   c) American slaves
   d) Chains

37. Compare the first sentence of the fourth paragraph with a simplified version.

Fellow citizens, above your national, tumultuous joy, I hear the mournful wail of millions, whose chains, heavy and grievous yesterday, are today rendered more intolerable by the jubilant shouts that reach them.

Fellow citizens, above your national, tumultuous joy, I hear the mournful wail of millions, whose chains are intolerable.

What does the simplified version remove from the meaning of the original?

a) The simplified version removes all of the author's anger toward the audience.
b) The simplified version removes the author's unwillingness to share in the celebration.
c) The simplified version removes the emphasis on *today* as a particularly bad day.
d) The simplified version removes the emphasis on the number of people in chains.

38. Why is the suffering of those in pain *today rendered more intolerable* than it is on any other day?

a) The 4th of July celebrates independence, which is ironic given that some people are enslaved.
b) The 4th of July celebrates independence, which is misleading because the nation was still under British rule.
c) The 4th of July celebrates independence, which the speaker does not know how to enjoy.
d) The 4th of July celebrates independence, which the speaker believes is not adequately celebrated in the United States.

39. In the last paragraph, the speaker declares himself *identified with the American bondman, making his wrongs mine.* Think of your answer to question 34 regarding the use of pronouns. Why does the speaker phrase his identification with the slaves in this way?

a) He can suggest to the audience that everyone hearing his speech is currently a slave.
b) He can show that all of those who are currently slaves can give sophisticated speeches.
c) He can show his sympathy with those in slavery but also show that he is not a slave himself.
d) He can voluntarily give himself back to slaveowners and begin working on a plantation.

40. Which of the following sentences best summarizes the "point" of the passage?

a) Paragraph 1, Sentence 2
b) Paragraph 2, Sentence 2
c) Paragraph 3, Sentence 13
d) Paragraph 6, Sentence 3

SUMMARY

We learn to read at a very young age, but becoming a good reader is a lifelong process. The skills introduced in this chapter don't tell the whole story, but they should get you started. Our main purpose in this chapter has been to get you to become *conscious* of a typically unconscious thing. Becoming aware of what you do you when you read can make reading more enjoyable and enlightening.

Words are powerful things. A single word can make all the difference. And just as a single word can change the meaning of a sentence, a single sentence can change the meaning of a paragraph, and a single paragraph can change the meaning of an entire passage. Whenever you are confused or lost, build your understanding by starting small. Writers want to communicate with you, and if you listen to what they have to say and how they say it, you will find that the rewards of close, careful reading are worth all the hard work.

ANSWERS

Sentences
1. c
2. a
3. b
4. a
5. b

For questions 6–10, answers may vary.

6. [Contrast because of the word *yet*] The band is one of my favorites …
7. [Contrast because of the word *though*] … they have not tested their results adequately yet.
8. [Contrast because of the word *however*] … it's later than that, and we're still waiting.
9. [Continuation because of the word *therefore*] This test is going to be really difficult …
10. [Continuation because of the word *nor*] … do I intend to pay good money to see it.

11. d
12. b
13. c
14. d
15. a
16. c
17. d
18. b
19. a
20. b

For questions 21–25, answers may vary.

21. *Seldom* indicates that Colleen does not go to her physics lecture very often, in contrast to the first sentence, which does not specify how often she goes.
22. *Eagerly* indicates that Rosita is excited to see her brother, in contrast to the first sentence, which says only that she is waiting for him.
23. *Already* indicates that the speaker had eaten the ice cream before, perhaps to suggest that he had not expected to, in contrast to the first sentence, which says only that the speaker ate the ice cream.
24. *Up* indicates that Henry vomited the chicken salad, in contrast to the first sentence, which says that Henry threw the chicken salad.
25. *Really* indicates that the speaker has had Chinese food that may not actually be good, in contrast to the first sentence, which says that the speaker has never had good Chinese food at all.

26. c
27. d
28. b
29. a
30. c
31. b
32. d
33. c
34. a
35. c
36. b
37. c
38. c
39. a
40. d
41. b
42. c
43. a
44. b
45. a
46. c
47. b
48. a
49. c
50. a

Paragraphs

1. b
2. d
3. a
4. b
5. d
6. c
7. b
8. d

9. b
10. c
11. b
12. d
13. c
14. a
15. d
16. b
17. a
18. d
19. c
20. c
21. a
22. d
23. a
24. b
25. c
26. d
27. a
28. a
29. d
30. b
31. c
32. b
33. a
34. d
35. c
36. b
37. c
38. b
39. d
40. c
41. d
42. b
43. d
44. a
45. c

Passages

1. b
2. c
3. d
4. c
5. d
6. d
7. b
8. a
9. b
10. d
11. c
12. b
13. d
14. a
15. a
16. d
17. b
18. d
19. a
20. a
21. a
22. b
23. d
24. d
25. b
26. b
27. d
28. a
29. a
30. c
31. d
32. b
33. a
34. d
35. b
36. c
37. c
38. a
39. c
40. d

The Essay

Author: Lori DesRochers

WHAT IS AN ESSAY?

In a book about reading comprehension, why is there an entire chapter dedicated to the essay? ETS and ACT, Inc., both ask students to write "optional" essays. Both of these essays require you to read and comprehend source text provided to you by the test writers. Thus these essays are far from simple "yes" or "no" questions or opinion pieces. Instead, each of these essays is a textual excerpt or statement about which students are to write an essay that takes into consideration the point of view of the author (or other individuals) and give a detailed analysis of that text. In short, you need to read and comprehend *before* you can even begin to write your essay. Since the first four chapters of this book very eloquently covered the skills you will need to improve your reading comprehension, this chapter will focus on what you can expect from the essays and how to use your reading comprehension skills to improve your writing.

HOW STANDARDIZED TEST ESSAYS DIFFER FROM ACADEMIC ESSAYS

In school, when you are asked to write an essay, your teacher doesn't usually hand you a question and ask you to provide a well-written and well-reasoned essay with solid examples in 40 to 50 minutes, but that is exactly what standardized tests are asking you to do. The SAT and ACT both provide you with brief source texts on which they want your commentary. They want you to demonstrate strong writing skills and effective use of language without having your paper reviewed or edited by others. This is a challenging task, to say the least. However, by working through the first four chapters of this book, you are well on your way to becoming a better writer; you understand how good writers structure their work.

Good writers don't just luck into their craft. They spend years—and sometimes decades—deciding the best way to convey their stories and present their opinions. They present an enthralling narrative or factual account of the event about which they want you to read because they have practiced how to do so. Bad writing is boring and redundant, and no one wants to read it, let alone spend money to purchase it. Why do graphic novels and books like *Twilight* and *The Hunger Games* fly off the shelves, while textbooks and other less-than-stellar novels sit, virtually untouched, in the dusty corners of public libraries? As you may have guessed, much of the popularity of books is due to their readability and the skill of the writers.

What ETS and ACT, Inc., are asking you to do in less than an hour is create an essay as compelling as *The Hunger Games* that is well reasoned and well written, and for this they will give you a very respectable score because, let's face it: the essay graders are tired of reading the boring novel when they could be reading about Katniss.

THE REQUIRED TOOLS

In this chapter you will be given some opportunities to practice your writing skills so that you can approach the essay portion of your standardized test with confidence and skill.

So then, what tools do you need to publish the next bestselling SAT or ACT essay?

In the space provided, write down some of the things you think are important for any standardized essay. Once you're done, compare your list to the one provided below detailing the important components that SAT and ACT graders look for in a high-scoring essay.

_____

_____

_____

_____

_____

_____

Here are some of the standards that the SAT and ACT cite as grading criteria for their essays.

SAT:

- Comprehends and demonstrates an understanding of the source text
- Is free of factual errors in text interpretation
- Uses textual evidence from the source text skillfully and appropriately
- Analyzes the source text, considering the argument and other stylistic choices of the author
- Contains appropriate support for the writer's argument from the source text
- Has a clear and concise central claim around which the essay is structured
- Uses a clear organization of ideas that is easy to read and follow
- Has a clear structure including an introduction, body, and conclusion
- Uses transitions logically and effectively
- Uses varied sentence and word choice

ACT:

- Understands the task assigned and maintains a clear focus on the issues of the prompt
- Addresses the multiple perspectives offered
- Provides a personal perspective
- Offers a complex and logical argument
- Considers the implications of a provided argument and perspectives
- Anticipates and responds to other arguments and counterarguments
- Uses a clear organization of ideas that is easy to read and follow
- Has a clear structure including an introduction, body, and conclusion
- Uses transitions logically and effectively
- Uses varied sentence and word choice

Were you surprised by any of their standards? Is the SAT or ACT grading your essay on items you never considered important? Were there items that you thought would have a big impact on your score but are all but absent from the list of grading criteria?

You may have noticed that several of the grading criteria for the SAT and ACT essay are identical. Those standards are mainly focused on the writing itself. The specific tasks for each essay may not be the same, but you will need to be an organized, effective writer who uses the conventions of written English well in order to maximize your scores on both the SAT and ACT essays.

Now that you know what the SAT and ACT are looking for in their essays and that some of their grading criteria coincide, let's look at the general skills that will help you write your "best-seller" essay.

Optional Doesn't Really Mean Optional

ACT, Inc., and ETS both state that their essays are "optional," but is that really the case?

For the vast majority of students, the answer to that question is a resounding "no." While the essays may be "optional" for the tests themselves, you also have to take into consideration the colleges and universities to which you will be applying. If even one of your potential schools is requesting the essay (and most of them do), then the essay is no longer optional. Notice we said "requesting" and not "requiring." When you submit optional information, you show willingness to go above and beyond what's asked of you, which could have a positive effect on your acceptance if the admissions department is on the fence concerning your application. So just remember, "optional" is not optional when it comes to taking the essay portion of the SAT or ACT.

A Note On Practice

Once you have decided to include the essay in your test preparation, the best thing you can do is practice the essay you will be writing. ETS, ACT, and The Princeton Review provide sample essay prompts with which you can practice your skills. Keep in mind that not all practice is equal. If you practice writing a bad essay, you are only reinforcing bad habits, not improving your skills and increasing your test score. You want to target your practice on the skills that need improvement and strengthen your ability to write an essay in an abbreviated timeframe.

The process needed to write an effective essay is largely the same whether you have two weeks or 40 minutes, but the abbreviated timeframe presents unique challenges. You will still need to start by understanding the task, brainstorming for ideas, and organizing those ideas to ensure a logical essay with strong support. Let's take a look at the steps for writing any essay and how you can squeeze them into your allotted SAT/ACT time frame.

Brainstorming

We'll look at the specifics of SAT and ACT essays a little later in the chapter. However, both tests will provide you with a source text to read and consider. They will then ask you to respond to that information in the form of an essay. Use the reading comprehension skills you acquired earlier in this book to analyze the source text so you can effectively brainstorm for ideas and examples with which you can write your essay.

Here is an example of an ACT essay prompt. Below the prompt is an example of what brainstorming may look like. Notice that there is no real structure to the ideas at this point. The point of brainstorming is to get the information out of your head and onto the paper as quickly as possible. Once you have the ideas on paper, you can organize them in a way that makes sense to you. And yes, we know, this will take time—and you have that ominous time limit weighing on your mind, making you nervous—but trust us, taking the time to organize your thoughts upfront WILL pay off in the end.

ACT-Style Prompt

Fracking is a process by which natural gas is extracted from hard-to-reach regions of the globe. Fracking is done by drilling a vertical and/or horizontal bore hole and then injecting high-pressure water and other chemicals into said hole. Injecting the chemicals, potential carcinogens, is the method by which the desired natural gas is transported to the surface for collection. While many argue that fracking has the advantage of driving down the cost of energy and providing a potential source of fossil fuels well into the next century, others are concerned about the detrimental effects of fracking on the environment, not the least of which are ground water contamination and potential earthquakes at and around the fracking sites. Since fracking affects several aspects of daily life it is important to consider the greater social implications that fracking has on modern society.

Read and carefully consider these perspectives. Each suggests a particular way of thinking concerning fracking.

Perspective One	Perspective Two	Perspective Three
The monetary advances of fracking are not worth the cost to the environment and human health. Contaminated ground water and ecological deterioration are not worth saving a few dollars on utility costs.	There are some advantages to fracking, such as lowering the cost of fuel, but in order to ensure that the materials used in fracking do not contaminate the surrounding area, a company should do everything possible to protect the environment.	More research is needed on the potential long-term implications of fracking on the environment and surrounding communities. Until such time as fracking can be considered safe it should be discontinued or limited to use in unpopulated areas.

Brainstorming Example

Me: Fracking should stop now, It's not safe, I don't want cancer, my friend survived an earthquake, what other bad effects does it have, what do the scientists say? Can they do it away from people to make it safer? What if they fracked in the ocean? Exxon Valdez, penguins, Tesla-alternate energy, solar panels are popular.

Pers 1—I like this, but what else can we do to get gas/oil, other forms of energy?

Pers 3—I doubt this will happen. Start a petition, protesters, is fracking helping anyone in its current state? What happens if we discontinue—war?

Pers 2—I can get on board with this, safety costs money, does it take away advantages of fracking, would companies do it, should companies make it safer, or just abandon fracking?

Again, notice that these brainstorming notes make sense to you, the writer, but another reader may not know what the notes mean or how they are to be ordered. As long as YOU understand what you have written, you are brainstorming correctly.

Below are examples of one SAT and one ACT prompt. Choose one to read and brainstorm for ideas on how to answer the question provided. (You can practice with the other prompt at a later time: for now just focus on one test prompt as you progress through this chapter.) At this point in the process, just write down brief notes on any information that pops into your head. Don't worry about whether your examples are good or make perfect sense—you can worry about that in the next step. Just get as much information out of your head and onto the paper as possible. You will come back and choose the best and most effective information in a few minutes.

Brainstorming Practice

Set a timer and spend 10 minutes reading and brainstorming for examples for one of the following essay prompts. If you get stuck, think about how another writer might approach the prompt. Think about the argument from the points of view of your friends, parents, teachers, religious leaders, or politicians. This will help expand your thought process and might suggest some examples you otherwise may not have thought of. For the SAT essay prompt, you also want to mark and label any of the items you see in the source text that fall into the categories noted in the task assignment, such as supporting facts and stylistic elements. Don't forget to use the task assigned to direct your brainstorming.

ACT Essay Prompt

With the advent of smaller and smaller cameras that are built into everything from computers to cellular phones to military and hobbyist drones, our society has become one almost obsessed with a pictorial record of everyday life. In the past only high-end businesses could afford the top-of-the-line security camera system, but now individuals with a little knowledge of computers can set up and survey their houses remotely, or even check in and talk to their cats from their smart phones. Facial recognition software can identify individuals in a crowded room, and friends and acquaintances can link pictures or videos to social media profiles. In many cases these pictorial records of life are harmless, but when they affect one's friendships and ability to gain or keep a job they can have detrimental effects on one's life. With everyone watching everyone else, are we safer now than we were when very little was being committed to film? Provided the ever-growing trend in recording every detail of one's life and modern society, it is important to examine the repercussions such a trend may have on individuals and society as a whole.

Read and carefully consider these perspectives. Each suggests a particular way of thinking concerning pictorial records.

Perspective One	Perspective Two	Perspective Three
Having such a public and permanent record of events can be very helpful for catching criminals, determining the true intentions of potential employees, and preserving memories that would otherwise be forgotten. It is important to keep as many pictorial records of events as possible to keep individuals safe and connected.	Allowing strangers to view personal events in one's life is a recipe for disaster. With just a few clicks of a mouse a complete stranger can gather massive amounts of personal information about another person. Because we ultimately cannot control who sees our images, we compromise our safety by sharing pictorial records of our lives.	One should be very cautious with one's image. Sharing one's life with those far away can help build friendships that would otherwise not have formed, but there is the potential for one's images to fall into the hands of those with nefarious intentions. Therefore, one should only share those pictures one is comfortable with strangers seeing.

Essay Task

Write a unified, coherent essay in which you evaluate multiple perspectives on the prevalence of pictorial records. In your essay, be sure to:

- analyze and evaluate the perspectives given
- state and develop your own perspective on the issue
- explain the relationship between your perspective and those given

Your perspective may be in full agreement with any of the others, in partial agreement, or wholly different. Whatever the case, support your ideas with logical reasoning and detailed, persuasive examples.

SAT Essay Prompt

As you read the passage below, consider how Hillary Rodham Clinton uses

- evidence, such as facts or examples, to support claims.
- reasoning to develop ideas and to connect claims and evidence.
- stylistic or persuasive elements, such as word choice or appeals to emotion, to add power to the ideas expressed.

Hillary Rodham Clinton—Remarks to the United Nations' Fourth World Conference on Women Plenary Session—delivered 5 September 1995, Beijing, China

1   Our goals for this conference, to strengthen families and societies by empowering women to take greater control over their own destinies, cannot be fully achieved unless all governments—here and around the world—accept their responsibility to protect and promote internationally recognized human rights. The international community has long acknowledged and recently reaffirmed at Vienna that both women and men are entitled to a range of protections and personal freedoms, from the right of personal security to the right to determine freely the number and spacing of the children they bear. No one—No one should be forced to remain silent for fear of religious or political persecution, arrest, abuse, or torture.

2   Tragically, women are most often the ones whose human rights are violated. Even now, in the late 20th century, the rape of women continues to be used as an instrument of armed conflict. Women and children make up a large majority of the world's refugees. And when women are excluded from the political process, they become even more vulnerable to abuse. I believe that now, on the eve of a new millennium, it is time to break the silence. It is time for us to say here in Beijing, and for the world to hear, that it is no longer acceptable to discuss women's rights as separate from human rights.

3   These abuses have continued because, for too long, the history of women has been a history of silence. Even today, there are those who are trying to silence our words. But the voices of this conference and of the women at Huairou must be heard loudly and clearly:

4   It is a violation of human rights when babies are denied food, or drowned, or suffocated, or their spines broken, simply because they are born girls.

5   It is a violation of human rights when women and girls are sold into the slavery of prostitution for human greed—and the kinds of reasons that are used to justify this practice should no longer be tolerated.

6   It is a violation of human rights when women are doused with gasoline, set on fire, and burned to death because their marriage dowries are deemed too small.

7   It is a violation of human rights when individual women are raped in their own communities and when thousands of women are subjected to rape as a tactic or prize of war.

8   It is a violation of human rights when a leading cause of death worldwide among women ages 14 to 44 is the violence they are subjected to in their own homes by their own relatives.

9 It is a violation of human rights when young girls are brutalized by the painful and degrading practice of genital mutilation.

10 It is a violation of human rights when women are denied the right to plan their own families, and that includes being forced to have abortions or being sterilized against their will.

11 If there is one message that echoes forth from this conference, let it be that human rights are women's rights and women's rights are human rights once and for all. Let us not forget that among those rights are the right to speak freely—and the right to be heard.

12 Women must enjoy the rights to participate fully in the social and political lives of their countries, if we want freedom and democracy to thrive and endure. It is indefensible that many women in nongovernmental organizations who wished to participate in this conference have not been able to attend—or have been prohibited from fully taking part.

13 Let me be clear. Freedom means the right of people to assemble, organize, and debate openly. It means respecting the views of those who may disagree with the views of their governments. It means not taking citizens away from their loved ones and jailing them, mistreating them, or denying them their freedom or dignity because of the peaceful expression of their ideas and opinions.

14 In my country, we recently celebrated the 75th anniversary of Women's Suffrage. It took 150 years after the signing of our Declaration of Independence for women to win the right to vote. It took 72 years of organized struggle, before that happened, on the part of many courageous women and men. It was one of America's most divisive philosophical wars. But it was a bloodless war. Suffrage was achieved without a shot being fired.

Write an essay in which you explain how Hillary Rodham Clinton builds an argument to persuade her audience that international women's rights are important. In your essay, analyze how Hillary Rodham Clinton uses one or more of the features listed above (or features of your own choice) to strengthen the logic and persuasiveness of her argument. Be sure that your analysis focuses on the most relevant aspects of the passage.

Your essay should not explain whether you agree with Hillary Rodham Clinton's claims, but rather explain how the author builds an argument to persuade her audience.

Organize

Now that you have your ideas on paper, look at what you have created. Think about each example you put on the page during the brainstorming step, and decide whether it is a strong example or a weak example. Will it be easy to write about, or will it take a lot of explaining before the reason it is a good example becomes apparent? Do you need to do more research before you have all the information you need to use this as a strong example? All of these things matter when you have a limited amount of time and space in which to write your essay, and no access to outside information to research your ideas.

Consider the following brainstormed ideas for the first ACT prompt in this chapter (page 194). Which of the following are strong examples, and which should be discarded because they are weak or hard to explain?

Brainstorming: Relevant Examples

In the blanks below, write whether each brainstorming idea will make a good example or a bad one, and why.

1. Fracking should stop now: _____

    _____

2. Penguins: _____

    _____

3. What do scientists say? _____

    _____

4. Exxon Valdez _____

    _____

5. Solar panels are popular _____

    _____

6. Protestors _____

    _____

7. My friend survived an earthquake _____

    _____

8. Tesla-alternate energy _____

    _____

Now look back at your brainstorming from the last section. Take a few minutes to select the most relevant information. Once you have decided what is necessary to put in your essay, take that information and organize it in some manner. Graphic organizers are a great way to take the chaos of the brainstorming process and organize it into useable information from which you can complete an essay.

Here are a few examples of graphic organizers. Choose the one that works best for you.

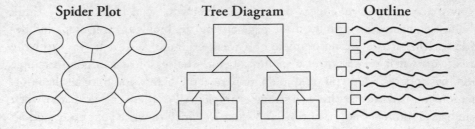

Here are two ways to organize the best examples from above.

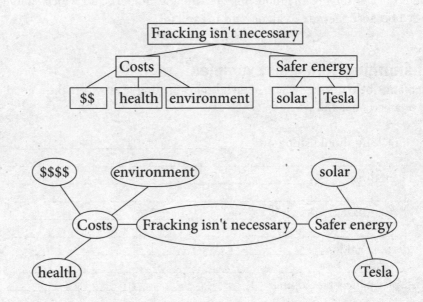

Notice how both of these graphic organizers note the main points and then connect to the important sub-points. Keep this in mind as you put your ideas together. Your graphic organizer should be the road map that leads you to a great essay; as such, it needs to note those things that are central to your essay. Use the task the essay presents as a guide in deciding what is central.

Now it's your turn to organize and structure your ideas from the last prompt into a list. Use one of the graphic organizers above, or another graphic organizer with which you are familiar, and arrange the strongest examples from your brainstorming into a more structured list that you can reference when you write your essay.

Essay Structure

Before you put your ideas into essay form, let's briefly discuss the typical structure of standardized test essays that receive the highest scores.

If you have written essays for your academic classes in the past, you are likely familiar with the five-paragraph essay structure: an essay with an introduction paragraph, three body paragraphs, and a conclusion paragraph. This structure can serve you well on the SAT and ACT as well. You will be responding to a different task for each of these essays, so we will save the discussion of exactly what should be in each paragraph for a little later in the chapter, but keep in mind that any well-structured essay transitions smoothly from one paragraph to the next.

An improperly structured essay is like the flight of which nightmares, or horror films, are made. You arrive at the airport to find your flight is running late and is oversold. The captain and flight attendants are overworked, tired, and not very helpful. You are eventually allowed on the crowded plane to find your seat, and after several failed attempts to identify whether you are even on the correct plane, you finally settle in a seat right next to the bathroom. Your flight sits on the tarmac for a long time. After takeoff, you notice that the flight map has your plane flying first north and then west before eventually settling into a southeasterly trajectory, which you hope will get you to your final destination. There is turbulence, it seems, from the moment you push back from the gate, and upon FINALLY reaching your destination you find that your bags have not made the trip and are patiently waiting for you in another country.

In parallel, a bad essay is littered with distracting ideas or has a significant lack of information. When the author fails to plan before writing the essay, s/he tends to write what comes to mind, relying on clichés and filler phrases to fill the page with words. In some cases, the author begins an idea and then leaves it unfinished because s/he has not fully determined how the idea will support the point of view, or the example does not tie back to the main idea of the essay. Some essays do not answer the question or answer a completely different question from the one that was asked. In some cases the essay says too much about one example and leaves another with a cursory explanation, making the essay feel lopsided or leaving the reader feeling as if the example was added just to fill space.

When essays are not planned, they tend to follow a "stream of consciousness," in which the author just writes whatever information comes to mind with no consideration for structure or flow. The author jumps from one point to the next and the reader is not able to follow the author's thought process, or perhaps the essay lacks a sound conclusion, or its conclusion introduces a new idea without explaining how it fits into the author's argument.

Conversely, think about a well-structured essay as a smooth plane ride. You enter the plane and find your seat easily, the pilot gives you a brief welcome and tells you how long the flight will last and that your in-flight movie will be *The Hunger Games*. Your takeoff is uneventful, your flight is relaxing, and you arrive at your destination in exactly the amount of time the pilot estimated, without encountering turbulence. You disembark after a brief "thank you" from the captain and flight attendants and find your bags waiting for you at the gate with a big red bow on top.

So, too, will a well-structured essay ease you into the body of the essay with an introduction paragraph that tells you what to expect from the rest of the essay and body paragraphs that flow smoothly from one idea to another (using transition words and linked ideas to avoid confusion). It ends without new information being presented in the final paragraph. The final sentence or sentences of a well-structured essay leave the reader feeling satisfied—the writer eloquently and appropriate sums up his/her ideas with a big red bow.

Transitions: The Smooth Flight to an Awesome Essay

Transition words are a small part of your essay, but they can have a huge effect on how your essay is perceived overall. Words and phrases such as "conversely," "in parallel," and "in addition to" help to show the links between your ideas and help the reader to follow your thought process. Transition words are words that connect one idea to the next and show the grader that rather than abruptly ending one idea and moving on to the next, you understand the connections between your ideas and know how to use the conventions of written English to demonstrate those connections.

In the space below, write as many transition words as you can.

_____

_____

_____

Here is a list of some effective transitions. Pick a few and use them in every standardized test essay you write. It may feel repetitive to you to use the same words in every standardized test essay, but the person grading your paper will likely only ever see one of your essays, so you don't need to worry about the redundancy.

Transition Words

SAME DIRECTION, or transition words for similar ideas:

Furthermore, Additionally, In addition to, Moreover

OPPOSITE DIRECTION, or transition words for ideas with disagreement:

However, Although, Instead, Nevertheless, Even though, Despite, In contrast

CONCLUSIONS:

Therefore, Thus, Consequently, Hence

INTRODUCING EXAMPLES:

For example, In this case, Similarly

Turbulence and How to Avoid It

Good Grammar

Anything you write, whether it be for school, standardized tests, or simply communication between friends and family, needs to have some context for what the words mean. You don't have the option of using your facial expressions or hand gestures in an e-mail to make your point clear. While emoticons and emoji help make casual communication more colorful, pictures will not go over well with SAT and ACT graders even if you are the next Hayao Miyazaki.

So, how then, can you communicate the most appropriate and effective meaning without the conveniences of modern technology? Go old school, of course; dust off the rules of grammar you learned in grade school and take them out for a spin. You have reviewed many of them already in this book, but here are a few additional examples of how to make your writing pop.

- No more YOLO and UR. (But you already knew that, right?) Don't use abbreviations in your essay. Write out as much as possible. The graders know you are in a time crunch so an abbreviation like USA for United States of America will likely not raise any red flags, but using text abbreviations, like UR or OMG, throughout your essay is a surefire way to make your score plummet.
- Know the difference between commonly misused words like:
  - *Your* (shows possession) and *you're* (contraction of *you are*)
  - *Its* (shows possession) and *it's* (contraction of *it is*)
  - *There* (a place), *their* (shows possession), and *they're* (contraction of *they are*)
  - *Loose* (not tight) and *lose* (to misplace)
  - *Allot* (to distribute) and *a lot* (a large quantity—and yes this is TWO words!)
  - *Two* (2), *to* (a preposition expressing motion or the person/thing affected), and *too* (also)

Grammar Practice

Correct the following sentences so that they are appropriate for an essay.

1. This is UR house.

   _____

2. Its unclear whether the forks belong on the right or left side of the plate.

   _____

3. She wanted too tell her mom that she <3'd her.

   _____

4. I LOL'd when you're shoelace was lose; U looked silly hopping on one foot.

   _____

5. Consumers do want cheap forms of NRG, but they also want to exist long enough to see that NRG be used for the GR8R good.

   _____

6. W/ appeal to emotion and historical precedence woven tightly w/ the current violations and injustices to human rights, Ms. Clinton is CR8ing camaraderie with her words, and in such strengthening the army with which leaders and citizens alike will fight this "bloodless war" for equality in human rights.

_____

_____

_____

Use Hard Vocabulary ... PROPERLY

There is nothing worse than reading a well-written essay strewn with hard vocabulary words used in an obviously wrong manner. To the graders it appears that you have just thrown in some hard-looking words to make yourself seem like a better writer. Don't do this to yourself. If you know how to use arcane vocabulary, go for it, but be sure you are using it properly; otherwise, stick to the words you know. Big words used well give you an edge, but big words used badly are the bane of a good essay score.

Review the following two examples, both of which are intended to have the same meaning. One is written with more complex sentence structure, but with inappropriate vocabulary, and the other is the more basic form of the sentence, but the words are all used correctly. The definitions of the "hard" words are provided below for your reference.

- The excursion of women from the political proceed is part of the reason that women's rights are so frequently valance, seemingly, without recuse, according to Ms. Clinton.
- Women are not included in politics. This is a reason that women's rights are frequently ignored. Those who ignore these rights do so without seeming to feel bad about the situation.

Definitions:

- arcane—known or understood only by a few
- bane—something that ruins or spoils
- nonsensical—something that does not make sense
- excursion—an outing or trip
- proceed—to move forward
- valance—a short curtain
- recuse—to reject, challenge, or disqualify because of a bias

Vary Your Sentence Structure

Know what a semi-colon, colon, and dash do in a sentence.

- A semi-colon is used to connect to related ideas that are complete sentences themselves.
  - Example: She went to the store; she picked up some milk.
- A colon is used after a complete thought and before an explanatory statement or list.
  - Example: The trek to the top of Mount Everest was harrowing: the atmosphere was thin, the path was rocky and washed out in many places, and the Sherpa guides would not take us the last two miles to the summit.
- Dashes can be used in place of commas on either side of dependent clauses.
  - Example: The cat—who was covered in dust—woke me early by meowing loudly outside my window.

Semi-colon, Colon, and Dash Practice

Here are a few sentences that are written without the punctuations listed above. How could you correct these sentences to show varied sentence structure? Check your answers at the end of the chapter.

1. She went to the dance she wore the corsage her date brought for her.
2. Aubrie ran faster than her teammates Kea and Bera to claim the school record in the hundred-meter dash.
3. The school play contained several elements that made it very impressive well-timed comedy, intense dramatic emotions, and writing that was true to life.
4. I told Lila my best friend about the date I went on last night.
5. Reading is my favorite pastime I complete at least one book a week.
6. When in Rome, do as the Romans do visit the Vatican, sample the pasta, and throw a penny in the Fountain of Trevi.

What You Already Know

In the first four chapters of this book, you analyzed how a good writer writes. You looked at parts of speech, appropriate word choice, and sentence and paragraph structure and how they fit into a whole passage, and analyzed how to find meaning in difficult passages. All of these skills are obviously reading comprehension skills, but they are also *writing* skills: when you think about why an author chooses words and phrases and presents them in a certain way, it helps you to determine a good way to present your own ideas.

Practice

Imagine trying to persuade someone to take your side in the following argument: **All schools, public and private, should require students to wear uniforms.**

How would you structure your response? What important items need to be present in your writing to make your argument effective? How might your audience respond, and how could your counter those arguments?

Below are some potential responses to the above statement. On the lines provided, write your counter-argument to the opinion presented.

1. Uniforms are a great idea because they eliminate the individuality that ultimately leads to bullying in schools.

    _____

    _____

    _____

2. Uniforms are a horrible idea because they restrict the individuality that allows students to define themselves among their friends.

    _____

    _____

    _____

3. Uniforms can be a source of school pride, allowing students' to identify like-minded peers from a distance, but they can also lead to cliques and the inability to make new friends because of an arbitrary geographic sense of pride.

    _____

    _____

    _____

THE SAT ESSAY

What It Looks Like

You have already seen the typical structure of an SAT essay in the beginning of this chapter. You will be provided with an argument from a speech or other historical document and asked to analyze how the author has structured the argument he or she is making and how effective it is. You are NOT being asked to present an opinion piece.

The Task

ETS says that the essay will show colleges that "students can demonstrate college and career readiness proficiency in producing a cogent and clear written analysis using evidence drawn from an appropriately challenging source text written for a broad audience."

What ETS is really saying is simply this: Students will read a persuasive essay and then use details from what they have read to explain how the author builds and supports his/her argument.

So, now that we know what ETS wants us to do, let's look at what they are going to ask you to analyze.

The task ETS assigns to you is consistent from one essay to the next. Only the source text will change. ETS asks you to consider:

- evidence, such as facts or examples, to support claims.
- reasoning to develop ideas and to connect claims and evidence.
- stylistic or persuasive elements, such as word choice or appeals to emotion, to add power to the ideas expressed.

ETS will provide a source text here for you to read and analyze.

Write an essay in which you explain how [the author] builds an argument to persuade [his/her] audience that [the author's claim]. In your essay, analyze how [the author] uses one of more of the features listed above (or features of your own choice) to strengthen the logic and persuasiveness of [his/her] argument. Be sure that your analysis focuses on the most relevant aspects of the passage.

Your essay should not explain whether you agree with [the author's] claims, but rather explain how the author builds an argument to persuade [his/her] audience.

How It's Graded

The SAT essay is graded by two readers on a scale of "inadequate" to "advanced" in three different categories—Reading, Analysis, and Writing—giving a total score of 2–8 in each category.

Let's look at each one of these categories in more detail so you know what you need to do to maximize your score.

Reading: To receive a score of "advanced" in the reading category, ETS is looking to see that you:

- Understand the source text
- Understand the central ideas and important ideas and how they are related
- Have correctly understood the facts presented in the source text
- Skillfully use evidence, such as quotes and paraphrases, from the source text
- Use the evidence from the source text to demonstrate understanding of the passage

Translation: You have to read the source text carefully and be able to identify the different types of arguments and persuasive statements that the author is making. You have to use the skills you learned earlier in this book to make sure you dissect the passage and understand the source text that is presented to you despite the structure or difficulty of the source text presented.

Analysis: To receive a score of "advanced" in the analysis category, ETS is looking to see that you:

- Demonstrate of an insightful and sophisticated analysis of the source text and analytical task presented
- Provide a thorough, well-reasoned evaluation of the argument in the source text considering the author's evidence, reasoning, and/or stylistic and persuasive elements
- Have relevant and strategically chosen support for claims made in the essay
- Focus on the most relevant features of the text that fit the assignment

Translation: When writing your essay you need to focus on the most important parts of the source text in regards to the task of analyzing the argument being made. You will need to determine which items are most important to the author's argument and use those to analyze how effective the argument was. In short, you need to stop and think about what has been said, and how others would respond to that argument.

Writing: To receive a score of "advanced" in the writing category, ETS is looking to see that you:

- Provide a cohesive essay that uses highly effective language
- Have a specific and accurate central assertion
- Include an introduction and conclusion paragraph and show a progression of ideas throughout the essay
- Use varied sentence structure, formal writing style, and objective tone
- Show a strong command of written English with an essay that is virtually free of errors

Translation: You need to write well. You need a structure and flow of ideas that makes sense and fits into the conventional style of writing following grammatical rules. The more varied and interesting your writing, the higher your grade will be for the writing portion of the essay grade.

What Else Do You Need To Know?

ETS has set the time limit of 50 minutes for the essay. That means you need to do all of the things listed above in less than an hour. How should you best spend your time? That can vary from student to student, so practice will help you determine how best to manage your time, but as a starting point spend at least 10–20 minutes reading, brainstorming, and organizing your ideas. Having a structure to work within is very important to creating a cohesive essay. Spend your remaining 30–40 minutes writing and revising your essay. Make sure your essay makes sense and that it is free of typos and omitted words.

What Are You Looking for When You Read?

According to ETS you need to identify the following when you read the source text provided.

- The audience to which the author is speaking, and why the author is a credible person to be speaking to this audience about this topic.

  What do you know about the audience to which the author is speaking? What relationship does the author have with the audience? Do the author and the audience share similar values, and if so, what are they? Does the audience have any sort of pre-conceived ideas about the topic which the author is discussing? How do the view and prior knowledge of the audience affect how they will respond to the author's argument or how the author structures the argument he/she is making?

- Why is the speech required; what historical context is there for this particular argument?

  Also look for the main idea, or topic of the source text and identify the intention or goal of the author as he/she speaks. Is the source text informative; does it place blame; is it trying to attack a perceived failing?

Analyze the Argument

When analyzing the author's argument you need to look at how the author is trying to bring the reader to his/her point of view. What sensibility is the author appealing to in order to bring the audience around to his/her way of thinking? Below are a few common ways authors will try to persuade their audiences.

Appeal to Credibility: A way for the author to establish trust with the audience. This can be accomplished by citing his/her credentials, or listing ways in which he/she is experienced in the topic on which he/she is speaking.

1. On the first day of class your math teacher tells you that by the end of the year you will be able to solve a very hard problem. What does she need to do in order to gain your trust and prove that she will be able to make her claim reality?

_____

_____

Appeal to Emotion: The author uses an emotion such as fear, happiness, humor, or disgust to build a feeling of connection with his/her audience.

2.   The author would like to build a feeling of camaraderie around graduating from high school. What kind of imagery should he use to connect with his audience?

_____

_____

Appeal to Logic: The author uses arguments based in facts and logic that will connect with the audience's own views.

3.   The author wants to convince you that the money you want to spend on prom is better spent elsewhere. What kind of logical appeals could the author make to convince you that this is a good idea?

_____

_____

Look for Support

When you analyze the argument made in the source text, you will need to identify any elements of style the author has used to bolster his or her argument. There are many style elements available to an author; below are a few common elements that you may see in the SAT source text. Become familiar with these items and keep them in mind as you brainstorm. Any place you can identify these stylistic elements in the source text is a potential talking point for your essay. If you are stuck in your brainstorming, start by looking at each of these stylistic elements and determining whether they are major or minor components of the argument. Major components of the argument are deserving of further brainstorming and commentary.

- Imagery—Any language that creates a "picture" or appeals to your senses.
- Allusion—A brief reference to an item, such as a person, thing, idea or event, or something that holds cultural significance.
- Tone—The attitude of the author or speaker towards the subject.
- Syntax—How words are put together to achieve a certain effect. First and last words can be significant.
- Diction—The choice of words in the author's statement.
- Comparisons—Comparing distinct items, and making a connection between them.
- Juxtaposition—Placing two ideas side by side in order for the audience to look at similarities and/or differences.

- Repetition—Deliberate repetition of a letter, word, or phrase to achieve a specific effect.
- Statistics or quotes—Using data or quotes from notable sources to support the argument by adding credibility.

Practice with Elements of Style

Identify any stylistic elements used in the following sentences.

1. The time for change is now. The time for action is now. The time to make a difference is now!
2. John Adams said, "Give me liberty or give me death." And so, too, shall we follow in his footsteps by storming the castle of inequality and breaking down the walls with all our might and energy.
3. The flowers presented to her were not just beautiful; they were so stunning her eyes welled with tears as she enjoyed the grandeur of what nature could produce.
4. As *Othello* lay open before me, my eyes began to wander to the Stephen King novel I had set to the side. Could these books really be written about the same topic: the betrayal of a leader?
5. The river lay before me as the sheets of an inviting mattress after a particularly intense football game. My tired body yearned to jump into the comfortable, silky smoothness, so I could relax and enjoy my summer in Montana.
6. As she walked across the stage at her commencement to accept her degree in veterinary medicine, she remembered fondly the proud smile her mother wore that day at the zoo.

The Well-Written SAT Essay: An Example

This essay is in response to the SAT Essay prompt on pages 198–199.

The powerful impact of Ms. Clinton's speech to the UN Fourth World Conference on Women's Plenary Session was heard around the world. Women and men will not sit silently while their rights or the rights of their brethren are violated. Ms. Clinton's eloquent speech put into words that which many women could not or were prohibited from vocalizing. She appeals to the leaders of the world—male and female alike—to bring marginalized people's, largely women's, rights in line with human rights. Through repetition of the facts, appeals to human decency, and analogies to historic events that have moved women's rights forward, Ms. Clinton's persuasive statements are directed not only at the women and leaders present at the Beijing summit, but also the many world leaders listening to her words that day. Stand up and fight for what is rightfully yours, she urges, we are here to support you, to help you find your voice and your rights as a human.

Perhaps the most necessary element that distinguishes a well-formulated argument from a mere exercise of rhetoric is the proper use of supportive evidence, of which Ms. Clinton's speech incorporates several examples. She notes historic precedent: "The international community has long acknowledged and recently reaffirmed at Vienna that both women and men are entitled to a range of protections and personal freedoms" and uses that as the foundation upon which she builds her argument. All humans, she orates, are ENTITLED to human rights, and she goes on to note that "no one should be forced to remain silent." The exclusion of women from the political process is part of the reason that women's rights are so frequently violated, seemingly without recourse, according to Ms. Clinton. But recourse, she says, will come. Slowly but surely, women will win their right to the decencies deserved by every human being. She says as much when she employs the example of suffrage in the United States: "It took 72 years of organized struggle" before women won the right to vote, but the "war" for women's rights in the U.S. was one of struggle but non-violence. By giving examples of this nature, Ms. Clinton is effectively saying to the audience at the Conference, *those of you seated here today, you can make a difference in this world. Start with small steps and speaking out, and you will be taking small steps towards the inevitable outcome.* Through her examples, Ms. Clinton shows that the process to secure human rights for all, women and men, has been set into motion. She is calling for a more "bloodless war:" that is, the process of equality for all. She is creating camaraderie among the diverse population before her and strengthening the resolve of those already interested in the cause about which she is speaking.

Clinton's mastery of persuasive rhetoric plays out not only in the evidence to which she refers, but additionally in the skillful use of repetition, and the way in which Ms. Clinton connects with her audience and uses her words to touch an individual's sense of right and duty. She uses words such as "tragically," "empowering," and "control" to elicit specific emotions in her audience. She speaks about controversial ideas such as restricted reproduction, families, and abuse to instill a feeling of urgency in her audience. Her allusion to "the right to determine freely the number and spacing of the children they bear" is a thinly veiled barb at the Chinese government's restriction of the number of children born to the Han people of China. Since the UN Conference was held in Beijing, China, Ms. Clinton is very adeptly noting local injustices that will ring true for a number of the important individuals present at the summit. She is relying on the aggravation of Chinese women at having their reproductive freedom limited by a misogynistic government, and enticing them into a peaceful, but not silent, revolution.

Ms. Clinton's speech shows many elements of great persuasive writing, but one element of a well-crafted argument is clearly missing: the acknowledgement of counter-points. Ms. Clinton very clearly makes no such consideration in her argument. This is a very strong message in and of itself. No, she says, lack of human rights is NEVER okay. There is no acceptable reason or logic that should lead one to think it is okay to oppress or abuse another human being. "It is a violation of human rights..." is used repetitively and with purpose to drive this point home. The strength of her conviction is contagious, and using her eloquent command of rhetorical skills, she is able to elicit feelings similar to her own.

The difficulty in dissecting Ms. Clinton's speech to world leaders reveals the skill of her persuasive rhetoric. With appeal to emotion and historical precedent woven tightly with references to current human rights violations and injustices, Ms. Clinton creates camaraderie with her words and, in so doing, builds an army of leaders and citizens alike to fight this "bloodless war" for equality in human rights.

SAT Practice

Now it's time for you to practice a few SAT essay prompts. A list of the most important ideas from each argument can be found at the end of this chapter to assist you in your practice.

Prompt 1

As you read the passage below, consider how Abraham Lincoln uses

- evidence, such as facts or examples, to support claims.
- reasoning to develop ideas and to connect claims and evidence.
- stylistic or persuasive elements, such as word choice or appeals to emotion, to add power to the ideas expressed.

Adapted from *Notes for Law Lecture*. Written about July 1, 1850, by Abraham Lincoln.

1 I am not an accomplished lawyer. I find quite as much material for a lecture in those points wherein I have failed, as in those wherein I have been moderately successful. The leading rule for a lawyer, as for the man of every other calling, is diligence. Leave nothing for to-morrow which can be done to-day. Never let your correspondence fall behind. Whatever piece of business you have in hand, before stopping, do all the labour pertaining to it which can then be done. When you bring a common law-suit, if you have the facts for doing so, write the declaration at once. If a law point be involved, examine the books, and note the authority you rely on upon the declaration itself, where you are sure to find it when wanted. The same of defences and pleas. In business not likely to be litigated,— ordinary collection cases, foreclosures, partitions, and the like,—make all examinations of titles, and note them and even draft orders and decrees in advance. The course has a triple advantage; it avoids omissions and neglect, saves your labour when once done, performs the labour out of court when you have leisure, rather than in court when you have not.

2 Extemporaneous speaking should be practised and cultivated. It is the lawyer's avenue to the public. However able and faithful he may be in other respects, people are slow to bring him business if he cannot make a speech. And yet there is not a more fatal error to young lawyers than relying too much on speech-making. If any one, upon his rare powers of speaking, shall claim an exemption from the drudgery of the law, his case is a failure in advance.

3 Discourage litigation. Persuade your neighbours to compromise whenever you can. Point out to them how the nominal winner is often a real loser—in fees, expenses, and waste of time. As a peace-maker the lawyer has a superior opportunity of being a good man. There will still be business enough.

4 Never stir up litigation. A worse man can scarcely be found than one who does this. Who can be more nearly a fiend than he who habitually overhauls the register of deeds in search of defects in titles, whereon to stir up strife, and put money in his pocket? A moral tone ought to be infused into the profession which should drive such men out of it.

5 The matter of fees is important, far beyond the mere question of bread and butter involved. Properly attended to, fuller justice is done to both lawyer and client. An exorbitant fee should never be claimed. As a general rule, never take your whole fee in advance, nor any more than a small retainer. When fully paid beforehand, you are more than a common mortal if you can feel the same interest in the case as if something was still in prospect for you, as well as for your client. And when you lack interest in the case the job will very likely lack skill and diligence in the performance. Settle the amount of fee and take a note in advance. Then you will feel that you are working for something, and you are sure to do your work faithfully and well. Never sell a fee-note—at least not before the consideration service is performed. It leads to negligence and dishonesty—negligence by losing interest in the case, and dishonesty in refusing to refund when you have allowed the consideration to fail.

6 There is a vague popular belief that lawyers are necessarily dishonest. I say vague, because when we consider to what extent confidence and honours are reposed in and conferred upon lawyers by the people, it appears improbable that their impression of dishonesty is very distinct and vivid. Yet the impression is common, almost universal. Let no young man choosing the law for a calling for a moment yield to the popular belief. Resolve to be honest at all events; and if in your own judgment you cannot be an honest lawyer, resolve to be honest without being a lawyer. Choose some other occupation, rather than one in the choosing of which you do, in advance, consent to be a knave.

Write an essay in which you explain how Abraham Lincoln builds an argument to persuade his audience of the proper actions of lawyers. In your essay, analyze how Lincoln uses one or more of the features in the directions that precede the passage (or features of your own choice) to strengthen the logic and persuasiveness of his argument. Be sure that your analysis focuses on the most relevant features of the passage.

Your essay should not explain whether you agree with Lincoln's claims, but rather explain how Lincoln builds an argument to persuade his audience.

Brainstorm and organize your essay in the space provided here. Then, write your essay on your own paper. Or, you may download and print out lined essay-response sheets when you register your book at **PrincetonReview.com/cracking**.

_____

_____

_____

_____

_____

_____

_____

_____

_____

_____

_____

_____

_____

_____

_____

_____

_____

_____

_____

_____

Prompt 2

As you read the passage below, consider how Lyndon Baines Johnson uses

- evidence, such as facts or examples, to support claims.
- reasoning to develop ideas and to connect claims and evidence.
- stylistic or persuasive elements, such as word choice or appeals to emotion, to add power to the ideas expressed.

Adapted from "We Shall Overcome," delivered 15 March 1965, Washington, D.C. to a Joint Session of Congress on Voting Legislation by Lyndon Baines Johnson.

1   Mr. Speaker, Mr. President, Members of the Congress:

2   I speak tonight for the dignity of man and the destiny of democracy. I urge every member of both parties, Americans of all religions and of all colors, from every section of this country, to join me in that cause.

3   At times history and fate meet at a single time in a single place to shape a turning point in man's unending search for freedom. So it was at Lexington and Concord. So it was a century ago at Appomattox. So it was last week in Selma, Alabama. There, long-suffering men and women peacefully protested the denial of their rights as Americans. Many were brutally assaulted. One good man, a man of God, was killed.

4   There is no cause for pride in what has happened in Selma. There is no cause for self-satisfaction in the long denial of equal rights of millions of Americans. But there is cause for hope and for faith in our democracy in what is happening here tonight. For the cries of pain and the hymns and protests of oppressed people have summoned into convocation all the majesty of this great government—the government of the greatest nation on earth. Our mission is at once the oldest and the most basic of this country: to right wrong, to do justice, to serve man.

5   In our time we have come to live with the moments of great crisis. Our lives have been marked with debate about great issues—issues of war and peace, issues of prosperity and depression. But rarely in any time does an issue lay bare the secret heart of America itself. Rarely are we met with a challenge, not to our growth or abundance, or our welfare or our security, but rather to the values, and the purposes, and the meaning of our beloved nation.

6   The issue of equal rights for American Negroes is such an issue.

7   And should we defeat every enemy, and should we double our wealth and conquer the stars, and still be unequal to this issue, then we will have failed as a people and as a nation. For with a country as with a person, "What is a man profited, if he shall gain the whole world, and lose his own soul?"

8   There is no Negro problem. There is no Southern problem. There is no Northern problem. There is only an American problem. And we are met here tonight as Americans—not as Democrats or Republicans. We are met here as Americans to solve that problem.

9 This was the first nation in the history of the world to be founded with a purpose. The great phrases of that purpose still sound in every American heart, North and South: "All men are created equal," "government by consent of the governed," "give me liberty or give me death." Well, those are not just clever words, or those are not just empty theories. In their name Americans have fought and died for two centuries, and tonight around the world they stand there as guardians of our liberty, risking their lives.

10 Those words are a promise to every citizen that he shall share in the dignity of man. This dignity cannot be found in a man's possessions; it cannot be found in his power, or in his position. It really rests on his right to be treated as a man equal in opportunity to all others. It says that he shall share in freedom, he shall choose his leaders, educate his children, provide for his family according to his ability and his merits as a human being. To apply any other test—to deny a man his hopes because of his color, or race, or his religion, or the place of his birth is not only to do injustice, it is to deny America and to dishonor the dead who gave their lives for American freedom.

11 Our fathers believed that if this noble view of the rights of man was to flourish, it must be rooted in democracy. The most basic right of all was the right to choose your own leaders. The history of this country, in large measure, is the history of the expansion of that right to all of our people. Many of the issues of civil rights are very complex and most difficult. But about this there can and should be no argument.

12 Every American citizen must have an equal right to vote.

> Write an essay in which you explain how Lyndon Baines Johnson builds an argument to persuade his audience that all Americans deserve the right to vote. In your essay, analyze how Johnson uses one or more of the features in the directions that precede the passage (or features of your own choice) to strengthen the logic and persuasiveness of his argument. Be sure that your analysis focuses on the most relevant features of the passage.
>
> Your essay should not explain whether you agree with Johnson's claims, but rather explain how Johnson builds an argument to persuade his audience.

Brainstorm and organize your essay in the space provided here. Then, write your essay on your own paper. Or, you may download and print out lined essay-response sheets when you register your book at **PrincetonReview.com/cracking**.

_____

_____

_____

_____

_____

_____

_____

_____

_____

_____

_____

_____

_____

_____

_____

_____

_____

_____

_____

_____

THE ACT ESSAY

What It Looks Like

You have already seen the typical structure of an ACT essay in the beginning of this chapter. In general, you will be presented with a source text on which there can be many different viewpoints. ACT will present you with three perspectives in addition to the source text. Generally, one perspective will be in agreement with the topic, one will be in disagreement with the topic, and the final perspective will straddle the fence on the topic. The essay instructions will then ask you to analyze these perspectives and provide your own perspective, which can be in agreement with any of the three given, draw pieces from any or all of the presented perspectives, or be a unique perspective. You are being asked to present an essay that contains your opinion on the subject but still incorporates and validates or refutes other perspectives.

The Task

ACT says that the essay should be unified and coherent, and it should provide evidence of evaluation of the relevant perspectives and topics presented in the source text. The essay needs to state and develop your personal perspective on the issue presented and explain the relationships between the presented perspective and your own. As you are analyzing the source text and perspectives, pay special attention to the strengths and weaknesses inherent in the different perspectives and why they may or may not be persuasive to others. When you brainstorm for the ACT essay, don't forget to include your perspective on the issue and the strengths or weaknesses your point of view may contain. Also consider the type of support you would like to add to bolster your own perspective.

How It's Graded

The ACT essay is graded by two graders on a numerical scale from "little to no skill" to "effective" in four areas: *Ideas and Analysis, Development and Support, Organization,* and *Language Use and Conventions.* Translated, this means that ACT is looking for an effective essay that is well-structured with a clear introduction and conclusion, and body paragraphs that use effective transitions to indicate the flow of ideas. It contains varied sentence structure and word choice and few grammatical errors. This essay also demonstrates a clear understanding of the task presented in the source text and presents a reasoned argument that analyzes the source text and different perspectives and shows how these ideas relate. It clearly establishes the argument of the essay writer and offers complex and logical examples to support the writer's perspective. The essay stays clearly focused on the task and is easy to read.

What Else Do You Need to Know?

How Best to Use Your Time

The ACT gives you a meager 40 minutes in which to plan and write your well-reasoned essay, presenting a uniquely challenging writing environment in which you have to read and analyze several arguments in a very short period of time. To help combat the inevitable stress that comes from such a short time period, practice is essential. In addition to the prompts presented in this book you can find additional practice on the ACT website and in Princeton Review material. By making the task of planning and writing second nature, you will be able to complete the initial phases of the essay-writing process quickly and move on to the part that actually earns you a grade: writing the essay.

It is important remember that ACT essay graders are looking for an essay that flows logically from one idea to the next, and the best way to make sure that happens in your essay is to plan before you write. Spend 5–7 minutes reading the prompt and the perspectives. Brainstorm any arguments that come to mind, and then place the best ones into a graphic organizer to which you can refer throughout the essay-writing process to make sure you are including all the arguments that you wanted to make within your response.

Throughout this initial phase of the essay-writing process, be sure to

- read carefully for and identify the main/important topic point(s) made within the source text and perspectives
- analyze the arguments presented in the prompt and in the provided perspectives
- determine your own point of view; do you agree with any of the perspectives presented or do you have your own unique view of the issue at hand?

Practice: Finding the Main Idea

Can you identify the main point the author is trying to make in each of the following examples?

1. Hundreds of thousands of songs are available for instant download or streaming, but many individuals still choose to listen to music on an archaic form of media, the record. These connoisseurs of music feel that this form of media gives a truer musical experience—connecting the listener more intensely to the emotions of the performer.

2. When it comes to cars, the faster the better. NASCAR is an incredibly popular sport because it draws on the primal feelings our ancestors experienced when reaching top speed while outrunning a threat, such as a cheetah or moose. The danger involved in the need for this kind of speed is what still gets spectators' hearts and adrenaline pumping and ultimately makes even the idea of fast cars exciting.

3. Peer pressure is a powerful thing. It can convince you that going against your moral compass is a good idea: Not even hypnotists have that kind of power over their clients, so why would you allow your "friends" to convince you that stealing or lying is an appropriate way to act?

Read and Analyze the Source Text

When analyzing the source text, identify the topic and the different sides of the argument presented in the source text. What has the author said and what are the possible problems or implications presented? Use the text below to determine the topic discussed and the assumptions made in each of the three perspectives.

Americans are pushing for more transparency in the process by which their food reaches their tables. Many U.S. foods still contain chemicals or preservatives currently banned by the European Union (EU) as harmful to humans. Farmers and the American food industry alike have argued that the EU is overly cautious and that the FDA has not found enough evidence to conclude that certain food additives are unsafe for human consumption in the amounts allowed in U.S. foods. Despite these claims, Americans are demanding more organic and raw, unprocessed foods, claiming that these types of foods, while generally more expensive than their processed counterparts, are ultimately better for human consumption and general health. As industrial non-organic farming methods come into question and organic foods begin to inundate the market, the cost of food and the health of Americans has become a social issue in need of exploration.

Read and carefully consider these perspectives. Each suggests a particular way of thinking about the relationship between processed and organic foods and the implications of such on health and monetary issues.

Perspective One	Perspective Two	Perspective Three
There are no known advantages to eating organic foods and no proved detrimental effects of eating traditionally farmed food. The cost of the organic produce is not justified by a significant need for such.	Studies have shown a reduction in pesticide levels in human blood after only a month of eating a fully organic diet. Any amount of deadly pesticides showing up in human blood is concerning, so despite the cost, Americans should eat organic foods.	Even a little organic food can have beneficial effects on one's health. However, the cost of organic food can be prohibitive for many families. Farmers should work to reduce the cost of organic farming to make organic foods more accessible to the masses. In the meantime Americans should consume organic foods when possible.

Read and Analyze the Perspectives

When analyzing the perspectives ask yourself what each perspective considers, and alternately, fails to consider. Is there anything that each perspective took into account or failed to take into account?

Determine Your Point of View

When determining your own point of view, first identify how you would respond to the argument and then consider how your argument fits with each of the perspectives. Are you in full or partial agreement with any of the perspectives, or do you have a wholly original perspective on the topic?

Examples

In addition to the above, ACT is expecting that you present examples to help support your argument. These examples can be academic, personal, or hypothetical. Examples are important inasmuch as they show that you have thought about the issue and considered the complexity of the topic being discussed. Be sure to include examples that could help support your opinion in your brainstorming. As you move your brainstormed examples into your graphic organizer, make sure to put them in a logical order to help you structure your essay before you write.

The Well-Written ACT Essay: An Example

This essay is in response to the ACT Essay prompt on page 194.

The state of the fossil fuel industry is constantly changing. The push for better and safer forms of energy are driving gas and oil companies to look for cheaper ways to extract these resources in increasingly hard-to-reach areas while keeping their profit margin high. The current approach to keeping fossil fuels ahead of the energy curve is the process of fracking, which reduces costs to the consumer, or so the fossil fuel industry would like us to believe. In reality, fracking releases into our environment harmful, carcinogenic chemicals that leach into our ground water and threaten to contaminate much of the United States' drinking water. When one considers that fracking sites may be located under populated areas, one has to ask, is the risk of even a small contamination of ground water "minor"? Is the cost of allowing the fossil fuel industry to cling to fracking really worth the risk of a cancer epidemic and potentially irreversible damage to the environment?

Proponents of fracking state that it is a very safe method to extract natural gas from otherwise inaccessible areas. They argue that the ability to locate and secure this fossil fuel allows the United States to ensure fossil fuel stores for the better part of the next 100 years. This, they say, will allow the citizens who rely on fossil fuels every day to heat their homes or commute to their places of business, which in turn will buy humanity time to gradually move towards safer and more sustainable forms of energy, such as solar and electric. Proponents of fracking insist that we need this technology and that, while there is some cost to the environment, methods are in place to prevent widespread contamination, and that the detrimental effects of fracking are disproportionate to the vast advantages that it affords the fossil-fuel-dependent first-world nations.

Others argue that fossil fuel companies should target their spending elsewhere. The trend among those that can afford it is toward more sustainable, environmentally friendly forms of energy, such as solar and electric. With the advent of Elon Musk's first fully electric, long-range car—the Tesla—it seems the demand for fossil fuels is going to meet its timely demise before the end of the century, assuming that costs for such technology can be lowered to the point of availability to the "average" citizen. However, proponents of "traditional" forms of energy are fighting back, making the path difficult for those who threaten to change the world for the better. Because Musk refuses to bend to the norm and use traditional methods of distribution for his cars—a move designed to keep costs and, in turn, prices low—Tesla is banned from selling cars directly to the consumer in numerous states. However, the argument still remains valid—consumers are moving towards viable, sustainable alternate forms of energy. The resistance of the companies supplying the traditional forms of energy also begs the question, what are they afraid of? Are consumers really so dependent on fossil fuels that we need a century's worth of fossil fuel in store? The answer to those questions is being silently answered by increasingly more common residential solar panels, and the popularity of hybrid technology. Consumers do want cheap forms of energy, but they also want to live long enough to see that energy be used for the greater good.

"Listen to us," come the cries of the general population. "We want energy that is cheap AND safe." Is the fossil fuel industry listening? Will fracking operations suddenly go quiet in the near future? That is yet to be seen, but the groundwork has been laid and the average consumer is ready to lead the nation in a demand for safe, reliable energy that will not damage the environment or the people living on the only planet that will sustain their existence.

ACT Practice

Now it's time for you to practice a few ACT essay prompts. A list of the most important ideas from each argument can be found at the end of this chapter to assist you in your practice.

Prompt 1

Ebola had an alarming outbreak in 2014 in Africa. This highly contagious disease spread rapidly in areas of Western Africa where health care is inadequate and many diseased individuals were from small villages where western medicine is still seen as some sort of magic or quackery. Those who seek help in western medicine may be exiled from their ancestral homes for seeking life-saving treatment, or, if allowed to return to their villages, are shunned. Knowing this, some individuals who came in contact with the Ebola virus chose to forsake their homes and risk flights to the United States or other developed countries where the survival rate for Ebola is significantly better than it is in the underserved region of Africa in which they resided. This helped to spread the disease to the Western world and start a scare in the United States that lead to many dissenting opinions on how to contain the Ebola outbreak. The slim rate of survival made the containment of Ebola an issue of global importance.

Read and carefully consider these perspectives. Each suggests a particular way of thinking concerning how to control the spread of Ebola.

Perspective One	Perspective Two	Perspective Three
Travel from Africa should have been officially shut down to contain the contagion within the regions in which it started. No persons should have been allowed to come or go from the quarantined areas.	All travelers coming to and from the affected regions should have been subject to immediate quarantine until such time as it could be proved that they were no longer carriers for the disease.	Travel should not be restricted in any form from the affected regions; instead we should track each traveler as they move about. Restricting travel from the affected regions restricts civil liberties and would have forced those suffering to seek medical attention by finding other, untraceable, ways of leaving the region. This would have made the outbreak worse because there would be no effective way to track the potential carriers of Ebola.

Brainstorm and organize your essay in the space provided here. Then, write your essay on your own paper. Or, you may download and print out lined essay-response sheets when you register your book at **PrincetonReview.com/cracking**.

Prompt 2

The introduction of the concept of a carbon footprint has many individuals looking to find ways to reduce their personal impacts on the environment. This has encouraged many drivers to move towards hybrid or fully electric cars, believing that these vehicles will help them reduce their effect on the environment. What many consumers fail to consider is that the process of creating these hybrid and fully electric vehicles has its own impact on the environment, one that may have a greater effect than a single fossil-fuel-devouring car could match. As the number of hybrid and fully electric cars climbs rapidly, the issue of their effect on the environment is an issue of social and environmental importance.

Read and carefully consider these perspectives. Each suggests a particular way of thinking concerning how hybrid and electric cars effect the environment.

Perspective One	Perspective Two	Perspective Three
While it may create a large carbon footprint to produce a hybrid car, the use of the car negates any detrimental effect that the creation of the car had on the environment. Furthermore, if the hybrid is used for a long time, the impact of its creation lessens even more.	The detrimental impact of creating a hybrid car can never be offset by the use of said car. Moreover, the disposal of the car's components, such as the battery, can have further bud effects on the environment. Hybrid cars are no better for the environment than traditional cars.	Hybrid cars and traditional cars both have an impact on the environment. The creation of hybrids requires energy and other potentially dangerous chemicals used in the creation of batteries. Traditional cars create emissions that are harmful to the environment. Determining which is the lesser of the two evils is not an easy task.

Brainstorm and organize your essay in the space provided here. Then, write your essay on your own paper. Or, you may download and print out lined essay-response sheets when you register your book at **PrincetonReview.com/cracking.**

_____

_____

_____

_____

_____

_____

_____

_____

_____

_____

_____

_____

_____

_____

_____

_____

_____

_____

_____

SUMMARY

In this chapter you have explored the essay-writing process and why it is important in the creation of a standardized test essay. Without the structure and organization of the brainstorming and planning process, your essay may fail to address all the tasks required by the assignment, or be unorganized and hard to follow. Planning will pay off in the form of a better essay, even though it means you have several fewer minutes with which to write the essay itself.

You have explored the tasks common to all essays and those specific to each of the SAT and ACT essays and practiced some of the those skills. Continued targeted and effective practice will help you to improve your essay-writing skills.

ANSWERS AND EXPLANATIONS

Brainstorming Practice

ACT Essay Prompt

There is no correct way to brainstorm, but keep in mind that you want to get as much information down on the page as possible. It doesn't matter whether your ideas make sense or have a structure at this point. Just get them out of your head and onto the page. Don't forget to brainstorm about your opinion on the prompt as well as why you agree or disagree with the other perspectives and how those perspectives relate to one another and to your potential perspective. Here are a few potential items on which you may have commented.

Perspective 1 may assume:

- that all pictorial records are helpful
- in general people are not bad, or do not have harmful intentions
- that pictorial records do not leave the hands of their intended recipients

Perspective 2 may assume:

- the majority of people have bad intentions
- individuals previously had control over where their images were used or placed
- that your image and your person are synonymous

Perspective 3 may assume:

- that one has the ability to be cautious with one's image
- pictorial records can facilitate friendship or relationships when individuals are separated by distance
- the connection made through pictorial record is a good connection
- people one doesn't know may use one's image in a bad way

SAT Essay Prompt

Answers here will be unique, but here are some important items relevant to the argument that Hillary Rodham Clinton is making in her speech.

- Use of repetition when she states, "It's a violation of human rights."
- The audience to which she is speaking is gathered to discuss the rights of women across the globe; much of her audience seems to be females who have a vested interest in the rights of other women.
- Ms. Clinton is calling people to action and appealing to their empathy and sense of duty and responsibility to humanity.

- She is using parallels to women's suffrage in the United States to show the struggle and the ability to do it in a nonviolent way.
- She is discussing the common ground of her audience—and all humanity—by discussing the rights all individuals should have.

Brainstorming: Relevant Examples

1. Fracking should stop now: Good—this is the opinion of the writer and is necessary to complete the task that is assigned by ACT in addressing their prompt.
2. Penguins: Bad—this idea seems to be without connection to the idea of fracking. It may need quite a bit of explanation to make sense to the grader and therefore should be discarded in favor of an example that is more clearly supportive of the student's response.
3. What do scientists say? Bad—while this may be a great point when you have time to research scientific opinions on the matter, in the case of a standardized test you will not be afforded the time to do research to support your opinion.
4. Exxon Valdez: Good—the Exxon Valdez is another example of how the risks of gathering fossil fuels caused detrimental effects on the environment, which is in agreement with the writer's opinion.
5. Solar panels are popular: Good—this will be relevant to argue that fracking is not necessary and will not require much explaining to link the ideas.
6. Protestors: Bad—this idea seems to be without connection to the idea of fracking. It may need quite a bit of explanation to make sense to the grader and therefore should be discarded in favor of an example that is more clearly supportive of the student's response.
7. My friend survived an earthquake: Bad—unless you are able to draw a relationship between fracking and earthquakes, this is hard to connect to the topic of the source text and opinion of the writer.
8. Tesla-alternate energy: Good—this has a clear tie to the need for alternate energy and seems to tie well to the solar energy example.

Turbulence and How to Avoid It

Grammar Practice

1. This is your house.
2. It's unclear whether the forks belong on the right or left side of the plate.
3. She wanted to tell her mom that she loved her.
4. I laughed when your shoelace was loose; you looked silly hopping on one foot.
5. Consumers do want cheap forms of energy, but they also want to exist long enough to see that energy be used for the greater good.

6.   <u>With</u> appeal to emotion and historical precedence woven tightly <u>with</u> the current violations and injustices to human rights, Ms. Clinton is <u>creating</u> camaraderie with her words, and in such strengthening the army with which leaders and citizens alike will fight this "bloodless war" for equality in human rights.

Semi-colon, Colon, and Dash Practice

1.   She went to the dance; she wore the corsage her date brought for her.

2.   Aubrie ran faster than her teammates—Kea and Bera—to claim the school record in the hundred-meter dash.

3.   The school play contained several elements that made it very impressive: well-timed comedy, intense dramatic emotions, and writing that was true to life.

4.   I told Lila—my best friend—about the date I went on last night.

5.   Reading is my favorite pastime; I complete at least one book a week.

6.   When in Rome, do as the Romans do: visit the Vatican, sample the pasta, and throw a penny in the Fountain of Trevi.

What You Already Know: Practice
Answers will vary; here are some potential counter-arguments.

1.   Not all individuality is a bad thing.
     Students will still stand out in other ways, so uniforms are not eliminating individuality.
     A robotic, compliant student is not necessarily a desirable outcome.
2.   Students struggle to fit in, and having a uniform takes the pressure off of students to have fashionable clothes.
     Students are able to define their individuality even when in uniform.
     Girls can add hair accessories or do their makeup in a certain way.
     Boys can add a different style of tie or shave designs into their hair.
3.   There is an assumption that students should have pride in their school, but it is possible that they attend a school not deserving of their pride.
     Students' looks do not determine their class of friends.
     There could be potentially dangerous outcomes if it is easy to identify a student from afar.

Analyze the Argument

Appeal to Credibility
1. Your teacher could show you her degree.

   She could teach you a similarly difficult problem and quickly teach you a process to make the solution very easy.

   She could show you testimonials from former students that address their initial skepticism and disbelief in their own ability to solve the problem and the subsequent ease with which they were able to solve the problem later.

Appeal to Emotion
2. The author could discuss an after-graduation tradition to which all students look forward.

   The author could use the imagery of hundreds of mortarboards being thrown in the air.

   The author could discuss the uncertainty of the future and the fears that the author and the readers have in common.

   The author could discuss his pride in giving a commencement speech.

Appeal to Logic
3. The author could remind you that the prom only lasts one night and that the average cost of prom is about $1000.

   The author could suggest other more practical items on which you could spend $1000, such as a car, or college books or tuition.

   The author could suggest that you gather several friends who have similar motives and suggest that you plan a less expensive way to have fun.

Practice with Elements of Style
1. Repetition
2. Quotes
3. Diction—the choice of the phrase "so stunning" to describe the flowers
4. Juxtaposition
5. Imagery
6. Allusion

SAT Practice

Prompt 1

Answers here will be unique, but these are some important items relevant to the argument that Lincoln makes in this source text.

- Reference to his credibility when he mentions that his failings are his experience.
- He uses repetition when he references the tasks a lawyer must complete and how he should complete them.
- He uses juxtaposition by stating that lawyers should "discourage litigation."
- He appeals to emotions: "Who can be more nearly a fiend than he who habitually overhauls the register of deeds in search of" things that will bring money to the lawyer's pocket—this is meant to bring a feeling of disgust to the honorable in his audience.
- He appeals to logic in the second to last paragraph by stating that lawyers are more likely to put true effort into their work if there is still something left for which to work.

Prompt 2

Answers here will be unique, but these are some important items relevant to the argument that Johnson makes in this source text.

- Johnson appeals to the emotions of the audience by calling on their sense of unity and nationality.
- He uses diction in the second paragraph when uses the words *brutally* and *long-suffering* and introduces a bit of juxtaposition when he notes that the protestors were peaceful and the assault was brutal.
- He presents historical precedent when he connects Lexington and Concord, Appomattox, and Selma, Alabama.
- He relies on feelings of pride and national identity throughout the source text, especially when stating, "the greatest nation on earth" and "we are met here as Americans to solve that problem."
- He appeals to credibility by using quotes such as "all men are created equal," "government by consent of the governed," and "give me liberty or give me death."

The ACT Essay

Practice: Finding the Main Idea

1. Some individuals feel more emotionally connected to music when it is played from a record.
2. Humans' desire and excitement for speed comes from our primal fear.
3. Consider why you might do things for your friends that are opposed to your personal morals.

Read and Analyze the Source Text

Answers will vary.

Main ideas:

- American food and food in Europe are regulated differently.
- Americans are concerned with where their food is coming from and what is in their food.
- The cost of organic food means it is not available to everyone.
- Food can affect Americans' health.

Perspective 1 Assumptions:

- There are no studies showing the harmful effects of non-organic food.
- If an advantage isn't proven it does not exist.
- The cost of organic food is too much.

Perspective 2 Assumptions:

- The study being referenced was performed properly.
- There are no other reasons that the study showed the decrease in pesticide in human blood.
- The cost of food is relatively unimportant (as it's not mentioned).
- The presence of pesticide in the blood is a bad thing.

Perspective 3 Assumptions:

- Eating organic will help improve your health if you are still eating traditionally farmed food as well.
- Farmers and distributors of organic food are interested in reducing the cost of organic food.
- Farmers have not already worked to reduce the cost of organic food.

ACT Practice

Prompt 1

Answers will be unique, but these are some of the important items presented in the source text and perspectives.

Main ideas—Ebola is a deadly disease that spread in part due to the exposed seeking more advanced medical treatment in other countries.

Perspective 1 may assume:

- Shutting down travel from Africa would have helped to contain the disease.
- Quarantines are effective for containing the disease.
- Entry of an infected individual into the United States would have increased the spread of Ebola.

Perspective 2 may assume:

- Quarantine would have been affective in containing Ebola.
- There is a way to prove that travelers were no longer carriers of the disease.
- Entry of an infected individual into the United States would have increased the spread of Ebola.

Perspective 3 may assume:

- That tracking of all exposed persons was possible via travel records.
- Infected individuals would not spread the disease to others while traveling.
- If travel was restricted there would still have been other, untraceable methods of travel with which infected individuals could have spread the disease to the U.S.

Prompt 2

Answers will be unique, but these are some of the important items presented in the source text and perspectives.

Main ideas—Hybrid and electric vehicles may not be as advantageous to the environment as many consumers believe. There are other potentially other effects on the environment due to the creation of these vehicles that may not be offset by their more environmentally friendly emissions.

Perspective 1 may assume:

- There are no environmental issues created by the disposal of the hybrid car.
- Individuals will keep their cars for amounts of time long enough to offset the environmental damage done during their creation.
- There is a way to reverse environmental damage by not creating more damage.

Perspective 2 may assume:

- There is no environmentally responsible way in which to dispose of the components of a hybrid or fully electric car.
- The bad effects of the creation and disposal of a hybrid are equal to or worse than those for a traditional car.

Perspective 3 may assume:

- That it is possible to determine the effect of each type of car on the environment.
- That the research to determine which type of car has a greater overall impact does not already exist.

About the Authors

Elizabeth Owens has been teaching and tutoring for The Princeton Review since 2004. Elizabeth, a former North Carolina Teaching Fellow, teaches test prep for the ACT, SAT, PSAT, GRE, GMAT, and MCAT Verbal, and advises students as a TPR College Admissions Counselor. Elizabeth loves to read, bake cookies, and play with her two young children.

Lisa Mayo has been working with The Princeton Review since 2004 and teaches test-taking techniques for the SAT, ACT, GRE, GMAT, LSAT, MCAT Physics, and SAT Subject tests. She graduated from Smith College and has a B.A. in Physics. When Lisa is not in the classroom or writing test questions, she enjoys traveling, reading, and snorkeling.

Alice Swan teaches ACT, SAT, GRE, GMAT, MCAT Verbal, and TOEFL for The Princeton Review. She holds degrees in art history from the University of Michigan, University of Chicago, and Johns Hopkins University. She lives in Evanston, Illinois with her husband and two sons. When Alice isn't helping students improve their test-taking skills, she can frequently be found knitting, gardening, baking, or enjoying the Lake Michigan beaches.

Brian Becker has been working with The Princeton Review since 2005, and he has contributed to preparation materials for the ACT, SAT, PSAT, and the GRE Subject Test in Literature. Brian is currently completing his Ph.D. in English at Rutgers, The State University of New Jersey, where he specializes in American Literature from 1865 to 1945 and in pedagogies of writing. Brian enjoys reading, traveling, writing, and playing squash.

Lori DesRochers joined The Princeton Review in 2008, and currently teaches SAT, ACT, GRE, GMAT, MCAT Verbal, SAT Subject tests, College Admissions Counseling and Early Edge. She also had the privilege of teaching for The Princeton Review in Taiwan. She earned a degree in Mathematics Education and Theater at Elizabethtown College, and currently resides in New Jersey with her husband and daughter. She loves spending time with her family, hiking, and traveling; she has visited 15 countries and 23 states and hopes to add more destinations to the list soon.

NOTES

International Offices Listing

China (Beijing)
1501 Building A,
Disanji Creative Zone,
No.66 West Section of North 4th Ring Road Beijing
Tel: +86-10-62684481/2/3
Email: tprkor01@chol.com
Website: www.tprbeijing.com

China (Shanghai)
1010 Kaixuan Road
Building B, 5/F
Changning District, Shanghai, China 200052
Sara Beattie, Owner: Email: sbeattie@sarabeattie.com
Tel: +86-21-5108-2798
Fax: +86-21-6386-1039
Website: www.princetonreviewshanghai.com

Hong Kong
5th Floor, Yardley Commercial Building
1-6 Connaught Road West, Sheung Wan, Hong Kong
(MTR Exit C)
Sara Beattie, Owner: Email: sbeattie@sarabeattie.com
Tel: +852-2507-9380
Fax: +852-2827-4630
Website: www.princetonreviewhk.com

India (Mumbai)
Score Plus Academy
Office No.15, Fifth Floor
Manek Mahal 90
Veer Nariman Road
Next to Hotel Ambassador
Churchgate, Mumbai 400020
Maharashtra, India
Ritu Kalwani: Email: director@score-plus.com
Tel: + 91 22 22846801 / 39 / 41
Website: www.score-plus.com

India (New Delhi)
South Extension
K-16, Upper Ground Floor
South Extension Part–1,
New Delhi-110049
Aradhana Mahna: aradhana@manyagroup.com
Monisha Banerjee: monisha@manyagroup.com
Ruchi Tomar: ruchi.tomar@manyagroup.com
Rishi Josan: Rishi.josan@manyagroup.com
Vishal Goswamy: vishal.goswamy@manyagroup.com
Tel: +91-11-64501603/ 4, +91-11-65028379
Website: www.manyagroup.com

Lebanon
463 Bliss Street
AlFarra Building - 2nd floor
Ras Beirut
Beirut, Lebanon
Hassan Coudsi: Email: hassan.coudsi@review.com
Tel: +961-1-367-688
Website: www.princetonreviewlebanon.com

Korea
945-25 Young Shin Building
25 Daechi-Dong, Kangnam-gu
Seoul, Korea 135-280
Yong-Hoon Lee: Email: TPRKor01@chollian.net
In-Woo Kim: Email: iwkim@tpr.co.kr
Tel: + 82-2-554-7762
Fax: +82-2-453-9466
Website: www.tpr.co.kr

Kuwait
ScorePlus Learning Center
Salmiyah Block 3, Street 2 Building 14
Post Box: 559, Zip 1306, Safat, Kuwait
Email: infokuwait@score-plus.com
Tel: +965-25-75-48-02 / 8
Fax: +965-25-75-46-02
Website: www.scorepluseducation.com

Malaysia
Sara Beattie MDC Sdn Bhd
Suites 18E & 18F
18th Floor
Gurney Tower, Persiaran Gurney
Penang, Malaysia
Email: tprkl.my@sarabeattie.com
Sara Beattie, Owner: Email: sbeattie@sarabeattie.com
Tel: +604-2104 333
Fax: +604-2104 330
Website: www.princetonreviewKL.com

Mexico
TPR México
Guanajuato No. 242 Piso 1 Interior 1
Col. Roma Norte
México D.F., C.P.06700
registro@princetonreviewmexico.com
Tel: +52-55-5255-4495
+52-55-5255-4440
+52-55-5255-4442
Website: www.princetonreviewmexico.com

Qatar
Score Plus
Office No: 1A, Al Kuwari (Damas)
Building near Merweb Hotel, Al Saad
Post Box: 2408, Doha, Qatar
Email: infoqatar@score-plus.com
Tel: +974 44 36 8580, +974 526 5032
Fax: +974 44 13 1995
Website: www.scorepluseducation.com

Taiwan
The Princeton Review Taiwan
2F, 169 Zhong Xiao East Road, Section 4
Taipei, Taiwan 10690
Lisa Bartle (Owner): lbartle@princetonreview.com.tw
Tel: +886-2-2751-1293
Fax: +886-2-2776-3201
Website: www.PrincetonReview.com.tw

Thailand
The Princeton Review Thailand
Sathorn Nakorn Tower, 28th floor
100 North Sathorn Road
Bangkok, Thailand 10500
Thavida Bijayendrayodhin (Chairman)
Email: thavida@princetonreviewthailand.com
Mitsara Bijayendrayodhin (Managing Director)
Email: mitsara@princetonreviewthailand.com
Tel: +662-636-6770
Fax: +662-636-6776
Website: www.princetonreviewthailand.com

Turkey
Yeni Sülün Sokak No. 28
Levent, Istanbul, 34330, Turkey
Nuri Ozgur: nuri@tprturkey.com
Rona Ozgur: rona@tprturkey.com
Iren Ozgur: iren@tprturkey.com
Tel: +90-212-324-4747
Fax: +90-212-324-3347
Website: www.tprturkey.com

UAE
Emirates Score Plus
Office No: 506, Fifth Floor
Sultan Business Center
Near Lamcy Plaza, 21 Oud Metha Road
Post Box: 44098, Dubai
United Arab Emirates
Hukumat Kalwani: skoreplus@gmail.com
Ritu Kalwani: director@score-plus.com
Email: info@score-plus.com
Tel: +971-4-334-0004
Fax: +971-4-334-0222
Website: www.princetonreviewuae.com

Our International Partners

The Princeton Review also runs courses with a variety of partners in Africa, Asia, Europe, and South America.

Georgia
LEAF American-Georgian Education Center
www.leaf.ge

Mongolia
English Academy of Mongolia
www.nyescm.org

Nigeria
The Know Place
www.knowplace.com.ng

Panama
Academia Interamericana de Panama
http://aip.edu.pa/

Switzerland
Institut Le Rosey
http://www.rosey.ch/

All other inquiries, please email us at
internationalsupport@review.com